Get the **GRADE** ★

AQA AS/A2
Geography

David Redfern
Malcolm Skinner

Philip Allan Updates, an imprint of Hodder Education, an Hachette UK company, Market Place, Deddington, Oxfordshire OX15 0SE

Orders

Bookpoint Ltd, 130 Milton Park, Abingdon, Oxfordshire OX14 4SB
tel: 01235 827827   fax: 01235 400401
e-mail: education@bookpoint.co.uk
Lines are open 9.00 a.m.–5.00 p.m., Monday to Saturday, with a 24-hour message answering service. You can also order through the Philip Allan Updates website: www.philipallan.co.uk

© Philip Allan Updates 2010

ISBN 978-1-4441-1257-3

First printed 2010
Impression number   7   6   5   4   3   2
Year   2015   2014   2013   2012   2011

This book has been written specifically to support students studying AQA AS/A2 Geography. The content has been neither approved nor endorsed by AQA and remains the sole responsibility of the authors.

All efforts have been made to trace copyright on items used.
Front cover photograph reproduced by permission of Jean-Léo Dugast/ Still Pictures.

Printed in India

Hachette UK's policy is to use papers that are natural, renewable and recyclable products and made from wood grown in sustainable forests. The logging and manufacturing processes are expected to conform to the environmental regulations of the country of origin.

Contents

Introduction v

Unit 1 Physical and human geography 1
Topic 1.1 Rivers, floods and management 1
Topic 1.2 Cold environments 6
Topic 1.3 Coastal environments 11
Topic 1.4 Hot desert environments and their margins 16
Topic 1.5 Population change 20
Topic 1.6 Food supply issues 27
Topic 1.7 Energy issues 31
Topic 1.8 Health issues 36

Unit 3 Contemporary geographical issues 42
Topic 3.1 Plate tectonics and associated hazards 42
Topic 3.2 Weather and climate and associated hazards 46
Topic 3.3 Ecosystems: change and challenge 52
Topic 3.4 World cities 57
Topic 3.5 Development and globalisation 62
Topic 3.6 Contemporary conflicts and challenges 67

Answers to questions 74

Unit 1 Physical and human geography 74
Rivers, floods and management 74
Cold environments 76
Coastal environments 79
Hot desert environments and their margins 83
Population change 85
Food supply issues 90
Energy issues 93
Health issues 97

Unit 3 Contemporary geographical issues 101
Plate tectonics and associated hazards 101
Weather and climate and associated hazards 105

Contents

Ecosystems: change and challenge 110

World cities 114

Development and globalisation 118

Contemporary conflicts and challenges 122

Index 127

Introduction

How to use this book

This book has been written to help you prepare for the AQA AS and A2 examinations in geography. It should enable you to be fully aware of all that you need to know and understand for the course, and to appreciate the necessary geographical skills. It aims to help you develop your study skills, make your learning more effective and help you with your revision.

Modular courses mean that you could have examinations at different stages of your course, so you need to be prepared from the beginning.

The specification divides the subject matter into 14 topics, eight at AS and six at A2. At AS, two of the topics (rivers, floods and management, and population change) are compulsory. You must then study at least one physical option (cold environments or coastal environments or hot desert environments and their margins) and at least one human option (food supply issues or energy issues or health issues). At A2, there are three physical options (plate tectonics and associated hazards, weather and climate and associated hazards, ecosystems: change and challenge) and three human options (world cities, development and globalisation, and contemporary conflicts and challenges). You must study a minimum of three options, of which at least one must be physical and at least one must be human. This revision book deals with each topic separately in the order in which they appear in the specification.

The format for each topic is:
* things to learn
* things to understand
* key case studies
* questions that test your knowledge, understanding and application of skills
* answers to these questions

The AQA specification is examined in two modules at AS and two modules at A2. Units 2 and 4 are examinations that essentially assess geographical skills, including fieldwork. For further guidance on Units 2 and 4A you are recommended to examine the student unit guide (also published by Philip Allan Updates) for these two units. This book concentrates on the units that test subject content — Units 1 and 3.

Exam technique

Good exam technique is vital. You should not be short of time in the exams because the papers are designed to fit the allocated time. However, you should still be careful not to waste precious minutes. Use revision and exam practice to develop your exam skills, so that you can spend all the time in the exam producing quality answers.

Good exam technique is rather like a jigsaw of skills, as shown in Figure 1. Each skill needs to be developed so that they all fit together perfectly in the exam.

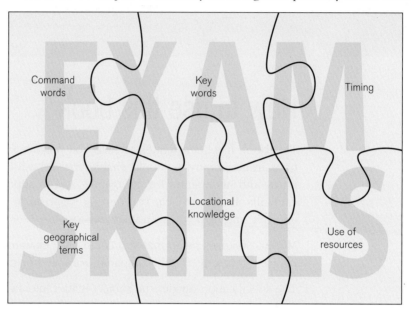

Figure 1 The exam skills jigsaw

Command words

Command words are instructions that tell you how to answer a question. Examples are 'describe' and 'explain'. A common cause of under-performance in exams is misinterpretation of a command word. One of the most frequent errors is explaining something when the question has asked you to describe it — in other words, saying 'why', when you should have been saying 'what'. This also happens in reverse, i.e. describing when you should have been explaining.

The table below contains a summary of the meaning of the main command words used in AS and A2 exams.

AS command word	Meaning
Define, what is meant by	State the precise meaning of the idea or concept. The mark tariff for this is usually low: you should give as many ideas as there are marks.
Describe	Provide a picture in words of a feature, a pattern or a process — for example, if describing a landform say what it looks like, give some indication of size or scale, what it is made of, and where it is in relation to something else
Explain, why, suggest reasons	Provide the causes of a feature, phenomenon or pattern. This usually requires an understanding of processes. Explanation is a higher-level skill than description and this is reflected in its greater mark weighting.
Outline, summarise	Provide a brief overview of all the relevant information

AS command word	Meaning
Compare	Describe the similarities and differences of at least two features, events, patterns and processes
Contrast	Point out the differences between at least two features, events, patterns and processes
Comment on	Examine the stimulus material provided and then make statements that arise from the material that are relevant, appropriate and geographical, but not directly evident — you are being invited to 'think like a geographer'
Justify	Give reasons why something should be done, and why other options should not
Consider	Describe (as above) and then give your views on a subject
Examine	Investigate and describe in detail
Annotate	Label a diagram, image or graphic. The labels should describe and/or explain features, rather than just identifying them (which is labelling). You should use several words for each annotation.

A2 command word	Meaning
Discuss	Give both sides (for and against) of an argument and come to a conclusion
Analyse	Break down the content of a topic, or issue, into its constituent parts in order to provide an in-depth account
Assess	Weigh up several options or arguments and come to a conclusion about their effectiveness
Evaluate	Weigh up several options or arguments and come to a conclusion about their importance/success
To what extent do you agree	After examining both sides of the argument, say 'how far' you agree with a statement option
Critically	Often occurs before 'assess' or 'evaluate' and invites you to examine an issue from the point of view of a critic — what strengths and weaknesses are there in the points of view being expressed?
Justify	Give reasons why something should be done, and why other options should not. At A2, each of the options available will have both positives and negatives. For the outcome chosen, the positives should outweigh the negatives; for the outcome(s) rejected the negatives should outweigh the positives. You should be able to explain all of this selection process.

Key words

Key words are instructions that tell you *what* to write about. They provide you with the focus of the question. They are often common words, but it is important to understand their meaning. Some key words are defined in the table below.

Key word	Meaning
Appropriate	Whether solutions are fit for purpose and realistic

Introduction

Key word	Meaning
Benefits	The advantages/positive impacts of something (social, economic, environmental)
Causes	The reasons why something happens
Challenges	Difficult, large-scale problems that require solutions
Characteristics	Key features
Concerns	Worrying aspects of an issue or problem
Conflicts	Issues over which two or more groups disagree
Consequences	The results of a change or process; they can be positive or negative
Costs	Disadvantages/negative impacts of something (social, economic, environmental)
Distribution	The geographical pattern, most often on a map. Look for areas with a high amount, a low amount, and anomalies within each of these areas
Economic	To do with money, work, industry, jobs and prospects
Effects	The results of a process, or an event
Environmental	To do with the environment, plants, animals, water, air and resources
Factors	Underlying causes of a problem or process
Impacts	Results of a process or change on people and the environment; they can be positive or negative
Interrelationships	Links between two or more features, such that changing one feature leads to changes in the other(s)
Issues	Views or concerns that some people may have regarding a feature or event, which may be beneficial as well as problematic
Lifestyle	The way in which people live their lives
Management	Using policies and strategies to minimise or reduce impacts or problems
Patterns	The distribution of something; where things are in a general sense — most often on a map
Political	To do with power: different viewpoints and policies, and the decisions to which these lead
Problems	Issues that worry people; the negative results of a process or change
Process	A sequence of events that causes a change to take place
Responses	Ways in which people react to an event — some may be as an individual, some may be as groups; some are planned, some are unplanned
Scale	An area of study — local, regional, national, global
Social	To do with people, their quality of life, health, education and prosperity
Strategies	Methods used to manage a problem
Sustainable	Being able to continue to do something without damaging the basis for its existence
Trends	The general direction of a change — rising, falling, fluctuating
Variations	How far something differs from the norm or average

Several key words operate in tandem and examination questions often use more than one key word. For example, many topics, when linked to key words such as problems, challenges, consequences, impacts, effects and issues have social, economic and environmental aspects. A further way to help you understand key words is to examine the geographical process.

Many of the topics you study fit into a sequence, as shown in the diagram that follows.

| Geographical issues begin with **causes**. **Processes** then occur which lead to… | …**changes** taking place. These can be changes to natural or human systems. The changes often have… | …**consequences**; these can be positive or negative (**problems**) for people and/or the environment… | …the problems and issues require **management** to find solutions and minimise **conflict** |

Locational knowledge

It is important that you approach the exams as a geographer and try to give a 'sense of place', especially when asked for reference(s) to examples or case studies. Exam questions often ask for 'locational knowledge'. This could be about scale:

★ global (world, worldwide)
★ national (country or countries)
★ local (small area)

It could be about levels of development, for example:

★ the developed world
★ the developing world

It could also be about type of place, for example:

★ an urban area
★ a rural area

The case studies you should cover for each option are made clear in this book. You should note that on this specification there are some *compulsory* case studies, so you should expect some exam questions specifically about these.

Extended-prose questions that require the comparative use of case studies are common. Much of the challenge of such questions hinges on selecting appropriate case studies. Make sure that you do not just write all you know about each study in turn. In planning effective answers to this type of question it is often necessary to interweave references to your chosen case studies.

A successful response to a question that starts 'With reference to a named…' requires:

★ choice of an appropriate example
★ detailed knowledge of that example in relation to the question asked
★ resisting the temptation to set down 'all-I-know'-type responses — you should harness only those aspects that are directly relevant

Watch out for questions that do not ask specifically for examples, but nonetheless expect them. The front of the exam paper usually says that you should illustrate your answers with references to examples and case studies.

Finally, it is worth noting that, especially at A2, the more contemporary examples that you include in your answer, the more you are likely to convince and impress the examiner that you have a sound knowledge and understanding of today's world.

Material of this nature provides the examiner with evidence of flair and insight — the best students will use it well.

Key geographical terms

Key geographical terms are defined in standard textbooks — examples include the terminology used for landforms and the processes that create them. You should learn key terms and be prepared to use them.

Key terms are important for two reasons:
★ If your geographical vocabulary is poor, there is a danger that you will not understand some questions.
★ If you do not use geographical terminology, your answers may be imprecise and expressed poorly.

Use of resources

You must take a structured and careful approach when using the resources you are asked to study in the exam. They contain key information that you will need to use to answer fully the questions linked to them.

Resources are used in two main ways:
★ Data-response resources should be used directly in your answer. This usually means taking information from the resource and incorporating it into your answer. Short questions are often data-response questions. Data-response command words include 'describe', 'state' and 'outline'.
★ Data-stimulus resources are used more indirectly. You might use the resource to get some ideas, or to provide a structure for your answer. Data-stimulus command words are more open, for example 'comment on', 'examine' or 'discuss'.

The range of resources you could be asked to interpret and use is extensive and includes:
★ photographs
★ maps
★ graphs
★ tables
★ diagrams

Timing

You should have enough time in the exams. However, you could get into difficulties and be forced to rush if you do not follow some guidelines:
★ Use past papers to practise timed exams. It is important that you understand fully the exam format and have some experience of working under exam conditions.
★ If there is a choice of questions (as there is in Unit 3, Section C), read all the questions before you choose which one to answer.
★ Be guided by the number of marks available for each question and the number of lines available for the answer. Do not spend 10 minutes on a question worth 3 marks, or 3 minutes on a question worth 10 marks.

★ As a guide, in Unit 1 there are 120 marks available and the exam lasts for 120 minutes. This translates as 1 minute per mark. In Unit 3, there are 90 marks available and the exam lasts 150 minutes — over 1.5 minutes per mark.

Revision: the final piece of the jigsaw

Few students enjoy revision. However, it is essential to review your work, learn it, and test your understanding. Every student has to decide his or her own revision strategy. However, there are a few rules that work for most students:

★ Revise in short bursts. For most students 30–60 minutes without a break is long enough. Beyond this time, you cease to take much in.
★ Try to do something active between revision sessions. Move into another room, take the dog for a walk, make a cup of tea, have a dance! The more you can take your mind off revision, the fresher you will be when you go back to it.
★ Just reading your class notes does not work.
★ Try to revise using as many of your senses as possible. Reading only uses one sense — sight. If you read *and* write, for instance by making revision notes from your file, you are using sight and touch. If you revise with a friend from your class and occasionally test each other or read out your notes, you are also using hearing. You might think this is silly, but driving is a complex skill that most students of A-level age can master quickly — partly because it uses most of your senses, and your brain then learns to assess these signals, which helps you to learn.
★ Revision involves taking the large volume of material from your course and condensing it into a form you can learn more easily and then recall in the exam. Your job is to identify strategies that will allow you to do this in the least painful way.

Some suggested revision strategies

1 Start by getting organised. Make sure your class notes are sorted properly. This is, of course, a long-term strategy. If your file is organised poorly, and the exams are fast approaching, then get help — borrow a friend's file or ask your teacher for help.

2 Plan your revision. Set aside days and times for all the subjects that you need to study, and stick to your timetable. This will allow you to continue to do the other things you enjoy, and fit in revision as well.

3 Set yourself clear goals. For instance, you might allocate one revision session to revising the causes of population change. Do not just open your file anywhere and start revising — make your revision structured and logical.

4 Make notes on your notes:
★ Use an exercise book or note pad because this will help keep things organised.
★ Break down your notes into bite-size chunks, using subheadings. This will make reviewing your notes easier.
★ Use numbered lists or bullet points. Try to pare down the information in your file to key points and important facts and figures.
★ Use different coloured pens to identify patterns and links.
★ Pick out key words and process terms, and write down their definitions.
★ Redraw key diagrams in a simplified way. You may be able to use these in the exam.

5 Make mind maps and spider diagrams:
★ Take a topic such as the impacts of climate change and make it the centre of a spider diagram or mind map.
★ Use A3 paper to give you plenty of space with which to work.
★ Break impacts down into a structure, such as social, environmental and economic, or developed world and developing world.
★ Next, use your file to add specific impacts to the structure, including examples, key facts and figures.
★ Spider diagrams can be a useful way to organise a mass of notes into something more coherent from which it is easy to revise. You could use them as posters. Glancing at them repeatedly will help the visual 'picture' stick in your mind, and recalling it in the exam will be easier.

6 Make your own flash cards:
★ You could use large post-it notes or postcard-sized pieces of card.
★ Flash cards are ideal for key case studies, key processes, key terms and definitions, and important diagrams.
★ As the space is limited, making flash cards forces you to include only key information. You will find you can condense your notes into something much easier to review.

7 Use your teacher:
★ Teachers like being asked questions. Make a note of any problem areas as you revise and ask your teacher to go over these in class.
★ Ask to do practice exam questions. You may not like these, but they are one of the best ways to revise and practise your exam skills. Try to look at some mark schemes so that you can understand how marks are awarded.
★ Ask to have regular tests on key terms at the start and end of lessons. This will make you much more confident in using the technical language of geography. These can be done using post-it notes — for instance, matching key words to their definitions.

8 Use your friends and family. Some students find they can revise with a friend, although this does not work for everyone. Revising with someone else has some advantages:
★ If you get stuck your friend may be able to help.
★ You can ask each other questions and test each other. This uses more senses, which helps you to learn.
★ Forcing yourself to explain a process or case study to a friend is a good way of learning and of highlighting areas on which you need to work.
★ Working with someone else can be more motivating, and less lonely, than sitting on your own trying to revise.
★ You could also ask your family to give you quick quizzes on key terms.

Topic **1.1** Rivers, floods and management

Things to learn

★ **The drainage basin hydrological cycle.** You should know the meaning of the following key terms: precipitation, transpiration, evaporation, interception, throughfall, stemflow, surface storage, overland flow, vegetation storage, infiltration, soil water storage, throughflow, channel storage, percolation, groundwater storage, groundwater flow (base flow), runoff.

★ **The water balance.** You should know the meaning of the following key terms: inputs (precipitation), outputs (runoff and evapotranspiration), water surplus, soil moisture utilisation, soil moisture recharge.

★ **The storm hydrograph.** You should know the meaning of the following key terms: discharge, base flow, rising limb, receding limb, lag time

★ **Long profiles and the factors that determine their shape; the progression to the graded profile**

★ **Valley cross profiles and the factors determining their shape**

★ **Potential and kinetic energy**

★ **Changing channel characteristics.** You should know the meaning of the following key terms: channel cross profile, roughness, discharge, efficiency, hydraulic radius, velocity, wetted perimeter, braided channels.

★ **Landforms of fluvial erosion: waterfalls/rapids, gorges, potholes, meanders and oxbow lakes.** For each of these features you should be able to **describe** the following: shape, size (dimensions), composition, its relationship with other features (its position on the river), and the detailed processes that formed it.

★ **Landforms of fluvial deposition: floodplain, levée, delta.** For each of these features you should be able to **describe** the following: shape, size (dimensions), composition, its relationship with other features and the detailed processes that formed it.

★ **The capacity and competence of a river; the spatial variations in load**

★ **The effects of river rejuvenation: knickpoints, waterfalls, river terraces, incised meanders.** For each of these features you should be able to **describe** the following: size (dimensions), shape, its position within the river system and the rejuvenation processes that formed it.

★ **The physical and human causes of flooding in general, including deforestation and urbanisation**

★ **The impacts of flooding in general**

Things to understand

In every physical section it is important that you understand the link between the shape/appearance of a landform and the processes that formed it. Taking the example of a river pothole, you should understand the following sequence of processes:

★ A cylindrical hole is drilled into the rocky bed of a river by turbulent high-velocity water loaded with pebbles.

★ These pebbles are trapped in slight hollows where vertical eddies in the water are strong enough to allow sediment to grind a hole in the rock by abrasion.

★ In addition, any small crack in the hollow is widened by hydraulic action.

★ As a result, the pebbles are gradually rounded and reduced in size by attrition. Potholes are found in the upper valley, which lies well above base level giving more potential for downcutting.

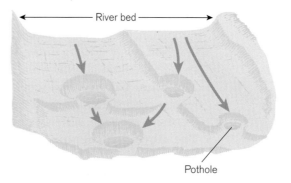

Figure 1.1 The formation of river potholes

The factors affecting water balance. You should be able to understand the interrelationships between inputs into the drainage basin, the outputs from the basin, the various ways in which water is stored within it, and the transfers of water from one part of the basin to another.

Factors affecting river discharge. You should be able to understand antecedent rainfall, intensity and duration of rainfall, snow, porosity/permeability of soil/rock, drainage basin size/shape, slopes, vegetation cover, land use and urbanisation.

Processes of fluvial erosion. You should be able to understand hydraulic action, abrasion, attrition, corrosion. You should be able to use alternative words to demonstrate you understand them — for example, scraping, scouring and rubbing for 'abrasion'.

> You must be clear in the meaning of these terms and of how they operate in a river context.

Processes of transportation of the river load. You should be able to understand traction, suspension, saltation, solution. You should be able to use alternative words to demonstrate you understand them — for example, rolling for 'traction'.

The Hjulström curve. This shows how erosion, transport and deposition are related to changes in velocity. It is a complicated graph, and you should be able to appreciate how differing river velocities impact on the load of a river.

Why and how rivers deposit their load. You should be able to understand the factors that cause rivers to deposit their load — for example, reduced gradient, reduced discharge, and variations in the size of load received.

The causes of rejuvenation. You should be able to understand the factors that cause sea level to lower, relative to the level of the land.

Flood prediction. You should be aware of how hydrologists try to forecast the likelihood of future floods, including magnitude and frequency analysis.

Flood management strategies:

★ Hard engineering strategies: dams, embankments and levées, channel straightening, channel enlargement, flood-relief channels (diversion spillways) and flood-storage reservoirs.

★ Soft engineering strategies: afforestation, land-use zoning and management, wetland and river bank conservation, river restoration and weather forecasting.

> You should be able to understand how each of these aims to control flooding in general.

Key case studies

★ The causes and impacts of river flooding in two recent events taken from contrasting areas of the world should be covered. One example could be taken from the UK or another developed country such as the USA (e.g. Mississippi flooding), and the other from a developing country such as Bangladesh or Mozambique. Make sure you examine the impacts from a range of aspects, such as social, economic and environmental.

★ Detailed studies should be undertaken of at least one flood-management scheme involving hard engineering and one involving soft engineering. Be sure of the relative advantages and disadvantages of each of the schemes you have studied.

Testing your knowledge and understanding

1 What is a drainage basin?

2 What are the inputs and outputs of the drainage basin hydrological cycle?

3 Explain what is meant in the drainage basin by 'interception'.

4 What do you understand by the term 'base flow'?

5 Study Figure 1.2, which shows a water budget graph (water balance). Which shading would you use for the area left blank on the right-hand side of the diagram (between the precipitation and potential evapotranspiration lines)? Explain your choice.

Hints

2 On a simple level, think of what is coming into the basin and what is going out. In terms of the water, work out where it might go.

5 What happens after the soil has reached field capacity?

> The **answers** to the **questions** are on pages 74–76

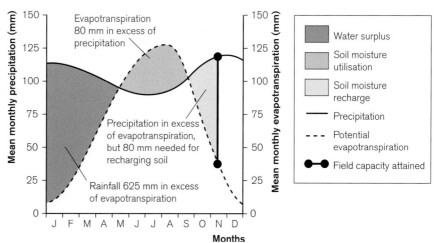

Figure 1.2 Water balance

6 How would you measure river discharge?

7 What factors can affect river discharge?

8 Study Figure 1.3, which shows a storm hydrograph for the River Calder on 6 July 2006 and answer the following questions:
   a What was the lag time?
   b How far above base flow was the peak discharge?
   c How did the steep slopes, impermeable geology and the sparse woodland cover of the Calder catchment contribute to the shape of the hydrograph?
   d What information on Figure 1.3 shows another factor important in the shape of the hydrograph?

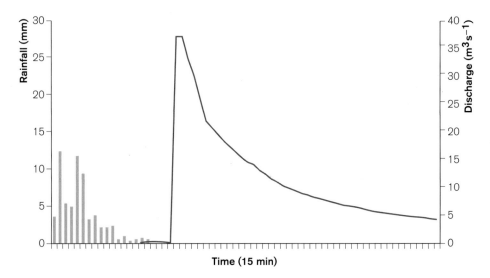

Figure 1.3 Storm hydrograph for River Calder, 6 July 2006

9 By which processes do rivers erode?

10 Define the terms 'capacity' and 'competence' in the context of river transport.

11 How do rivers transport their load?

12 Why do rivers deposit their load?

13 Study Figure 1.4, which shows the changes in sediment roundness on a section of the River Aire in Yorkshire.
   a Describe the changes in the roundness of sediment along the section.
   b How could the changes that occur around 8 kilometres be explained?

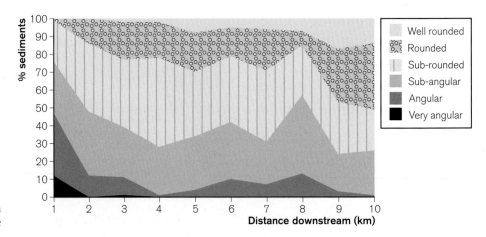

Figure 1.4 Downstream changes in sediment roundness on the River Aire

14 How can variations in the long profile be explained?

15 How does the changing shape of a river's channel affect its efficiency?

16 Calculate the hydraulic radius of the two channels shown in Figure 1.5. Which channel is more efficient?

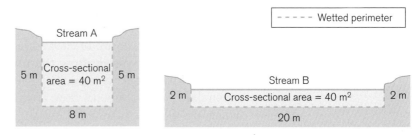

Figure 1.5 Channel shape

17 How does channel roughness affect a river?

18 Explain the formation of braided channels.

19 How do rivers form floodplains?

20 Explain the formation of a delta.

21 Explain what is meant by 'river rejuvenation'.

22 How are incised meanders formed?

23 What are the physical causes of river flooding?

24 How can human activities lead to river flooding?

25 How can floods be predicted?

26 Compare the impacts of a major flood in two contrasting areas of the world.

27 In terms of responses to a flood problem, what do you understand by 'hard engineering' solutions?

28 How are 'soft engineering' solutions better for a river system than solutions based upon hard engineering?

29 Figure 1.6 describes a major flood event, which took place in Hull in June 2007. What was the impact of the flood upon the city of Hull?

On 25 June Hull received 96 mm of rainfall in 2 hours, almost one-sixth of its average annual precipitation. This resulted in extensive flooding of the city, engulfing over 7000 residential properties and 1300 businesses. One person died. By 12 July, thousands of insurance claims had been received for flood damage to properties, at an estimated cost to insurers of £250 million, but it was estimated that 2000 families had no contents' insurance. The local council, in defiance of government policy, did not have flood insurance for its properties; some 3500 council houses and 12 schools suffered severe damage as a result of the floods. Special assistance was provided by the local council to those affected who were elderly or disabled and those families with children below school age, whether insured or not. £18 million was earmarked by Hull City Council for repairs to affected homes. For the first time ever, the national government agreed to pay compensation to uninsured individuals.

Figure 1.6

30 How may global warming affect rivers and drainage basins?

Topic **1.2** Cold environments

Things to learn

★ **The global distribution of cold environments including polar (marine and land), alpine, glacial and periglacial.** You should know the meaning of each term, the areas where they are to be found (both today and in the past) and the actual and relative size of each at the present time.

★ **The glacier as a system; how the glacial budget works and the types of ice flow within the system.** You should know where the following operate within the system: rotational flow, compressional flow, extension flow and basal sliding; the differences in flow between warm- and cold-based glaciers.

★ **Landforms of glacial erosion: corries, arêtes, pyramidal peaks, glacial troughs, hanging valleys, ribbon lakes and roches moutonnées.** For each feature you should be able to **describe** the following: shape, size (dimensions), position within the glacial area (i.e. its relationships with other features), orientation and the detailed processes that formed it. Know examples of the major landforms.

★ **The ways in which glaciers transport debris to include: on the top (supraglacial), within the ice (englacial) and underneath the ice (subglacial)**

★ **Landforms that result mainly from glacial deposition: drumlins and moraines (terminal and recessional).** For each feature you should be able to **describe** the following: shape, size (dimensions), composition, position within the glacial area (i.e. its relationship with other features), orientation and the detailed processes that formed it.

★ **Landforms that result from fluvioglacial processes: meltwater channels, eskers, kames, outwash plains (including kettle holes).** For each feature you should be able to **describe** the following: shape, size (dimensions), composition (if applicable), position within the periglacial area (i.e. its relationship with other features), orientation and the detailed processes that formed it.

★ **A description of the permafrost**

★ **The major landforms that result from the processes of periglaciation: nivation hollows, ice wedges, patterned ground, pingos and solifluction lobes.** You should be able to **describe** each feature in terms of shape, size (dimensions), composition, (if applicable), position within the periglacial area, orientation and link it closely with the processes that produced it.

★ **The traditional economy of the tundra and its recent changes/adaptations**

★ **Early resource exploitation in the tundra by outsiders (sealing and whaling) and recent developments in the area such as oil exploitation, fishing and tourism**

★ **The concept of a fragile environment and why the tundra should be considered as such; wilderness areas and why they are considered to be important**

★ **Sustainable development**

★ **Conservation, protection and sustainable development in Antarctica**

> This should, in particular, make reference to the activities of the indigenous population and how they formed sustainable economies.

> This should also include some knowledge of the Southern Ocean, the seas that surround Antarctica.

Things to understand

In every physical section it is important that you understand the link between the shape/appearance of a landform and the processes that formed it. Taking the example of a corrie, you must be able to understand the following:

★ initial hollow — formed by the process of nivation
★ steep backwall — result of frost shattering and plucking by ice
★ deep hollow — result of rotational movement of ice within the corrie and the debris obtained through frost shattering and plucking carrying out abrasion
★ rock lip — the result of the over-deepening of the hollow
★ possible moraine on lip — deposited during deglaciation as the glacier 'retreated' into corrie

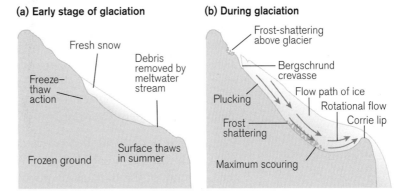

Figure 1.7 The formation of a corrie

Accumulation and ablation within the glacial budget. You should understand how the balance between the inputs into the system (accumulation) and the outputs (mainly ablation) affects the state of a glacier and its movement. You should also understand how, in temperate glaciers, there is a negative balance in summer and the reverse in winter.

Types of ice flow: rotational, compressional, extensional and basal sliding. It is important to understand how these types of flow occur and the impact that each has upon the work of the glacier — for example, erosion and deposition.

Processes of glacial erosion: abrasion and plucking. You should understand in detail how these two processes work and the effect that they can have on the glacial landscape. You should also understand how these processes are responsible for the features of glacial erosion such as corries, arêtes, pyramidal peaks, glacial troughs and hanging valleys. The detail expected is shown in the corrie example.

The process of frost shattering. You should understand how this process contributes material to enable a glacier to carry out the process of abrasion.

The transportation of debris by a glacier. You should understand the various methods of transportation (supraglacial, englacial and subglacial) and why material is carried in that position.

Glacial deposition. You should understand the difference between lodgement and ablation till and where you find each of these in the glacial landscape. You should also understand the formation of drumlins and moraines.

Again, it is important to understand the link between the detail of the feature and the exact process bringing it about.

The processes connected with fluvioglaciation, including the role of glacial meltwater. You should understand how fluvioglacial processes formed eskers, kames, kettle holes and the outwash plain.

Periglacial processes. You should understand how periglacial processes operate and, in particular, how they cause specific landforms. This should involve frost shattering being responsible for scree and blockfields, nivation for nivation hollows, solifluction for lobes, frost heave for stone stripes and polygons and ground contraction for ice wedges. You should also understand how wind and water action can affect the periglacial landscape.

Human activity. You should understand how people in modern times are able to cope with the difficult physical conditions presented by the tundra and how it can be possible for development to be sustainable.

Key case studies

★ Antarctica and the Southern Ocean, including the exploitation of the seas and the development of tourism should be covered. Contemporary issues should be considered involving conservation, protection, development and sustainability in this wilderness region.

★ Detailed studies should also be made of other aspects of human involvement in the tundra. Some suggested topics are the Trans-Alaska oil pipeline, the economy of the indigenous populations of northern North America and northern Eurasia, and the Arctic National Wildlife Refuge (ANWR) with particular reference to the oil industry.

 ## Testing your knowledge and understanding

1 Where would you find ice sheets at the present day?

2 What do you understand by the term 'snow line'?

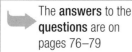
Hint

3 Try to work out which slope will be warmer.

The **answers** to the **questions** are on pages 76–79

3 On European mountains, on which side (north or south) is the snow line higher in summer? Explain your answer.

4 Explain the formation of 'neve' (firn).

5 Describe three types of ice flow associated with valley glaciers.

6 Look at Figure 1.8 which shows the effect of ice movement on a flexible pipe inserted vertically into a glacier. Using the diagram and your own knowledge, explain why the pipe has deformed in the way it has.

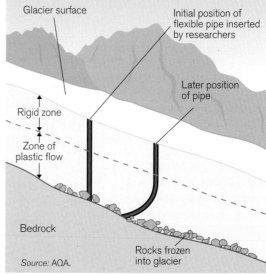

Figure 1.8 Ice movement

Hint

8 For **b**, think of the balance between snow accumulation and melting.

7 A glacier can be described as a 'system'. What do you understand by this?

8 a What is meant by the term 'ablation'?

b Account for the seasonal variations in the mass of the glacier shown in Figure 1.9.

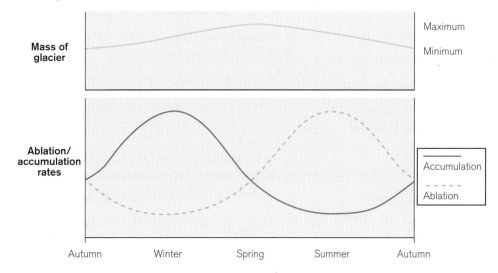

Figure 1.9 Seasonal variations in the mass of a temperate valley glacier and annual expected ablation and accumulation rates

Hints

9 Try to work out if more or less ice is created. Given an increase or decrease in mass, what will happen to the glacier in terms of area?

12 You should try to link all the detailed aspects of the feature identified to the exact process which formed them.

9 When losses (outputs) exceed supply (inputs) within a glacial system, what happens to the glacier itself?

10 Describe two ways in which glaciers can erode the landscape.

11 Describe the major features of a corrie (cirque).

12 Name the feature shown on Figure 1.10 and explain how it has been formed.

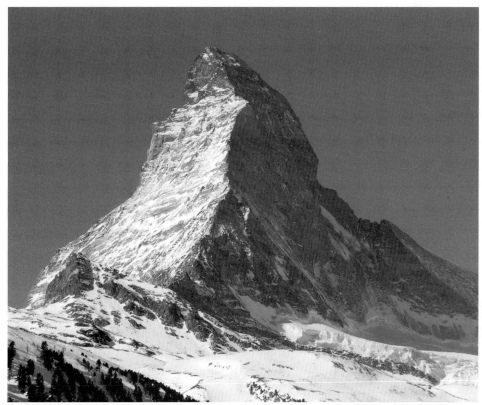

Figure 1.10 Matterhorn

Hint

14 Think of your answer in categories, i.e. shape, height, orientation, composition.

13 Describe the major physical features of a glacial trough.

14 What are the major differences between roches moutonnées and drumlins?

15 Where do glaciers transport material?

16 Where would you find:

　a　terminal moraines
　b　recessional moraines?

17 How would you distinguish between glacial and fluvioglacial deposits?

Hint

18 For **c**, think why a lake should have formed there in the past.

18 Figure 1.11 shows the typical features left behind on a lowland area after the retreat of a glacier or ice sheet. Study the diagram and then answer the following questions:

　a　In which direction did the ice advance?
　b　Which major fluvioglacial feature is not included on Figure 1.11?
　c　Explain the presence of the lake deposits.

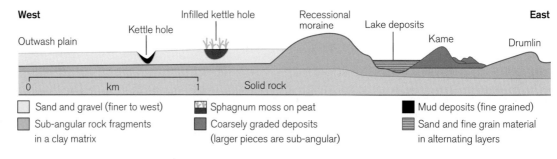

Figure 1.11 Features of lowland glaciation

19 How are outwash plains formed?

20 What is permafrost?

21 Explain the following processes:

　a　frost shattering
　b　nivation

22 What is the process of solifluction and how does it shape the landscape?

Hint

24 Why should any environment be considered fragile? Then apply this explanation to the tundra.

23 What do you understand by the term 'tundra'?

24 Why is the tundra considered to be a fragile environment?

25 How did the indigenous population of the tundra exploit their environment?

26 For what reasons has the tundra been exploited in recent years?

27 In modern times, how have people been able to cope in the tundra with the adverse physical conditions?

28 Since the early nineteenth century, what have been the major economic developments within the Southern Ocean and Antarctica?

29 How could tourism damage Antarctica?

Hint

30 First define what you mean by sustainable and then determine if the present development can be classified as such.

30 Is the current economic exploitation of the Southern Ocean and Antarctica sustainable?

Topic **1.3** Coastal environments

Things to learn

★ **Constructive and destructive waves.** You should know the differences between each of these types of waves, and the factors that cause them to be different.

★ **Tides.** You should know the main characteristics of tides and the factors that cause them to exist.

★ **Sediment sources and cells.** You should know their main characteristics and how they are identified.

★ **Coastal erosion landforms: headlands and bays, blow holes, arches and stacks, cliffs and wave-cut platforms.** For each landform you should be able to **describe** its shape, size (dimensions), composition, position within the coastal area (its relationship to other features) and the detailed processes that formed it. You should also know a named and located example of the major landforms.

★ **Coastal depositional landforms: beaches and associated features — berms, runnels and cusps, spits, bars, dunes and salt marshes.** For each landform you should be able to **describe** its shape, size (dimensions), composition, position within the coastal area (its relationship to other features) and the detailed processes that formed it. You should also know a named and located example of the major landforms.

★ **Coastlines of submergence and emergence and associated landforms.** For each feature (fjord, ria, raised beach, relict cliff) you should be able to **describe** its shape, size (dimensions), position within the coastal area (relationship to other features), composition, orientation, and the detailed processes that formed it. You should also know a named and located example of each landform.

Things to understand

In every physical section it is important that you understand the link between the shape/appearance of the landform and the processes that formed it. Taking the example of a stack, you must be able to understand the following sequence of events (see Figure 1.12):

★ initial **cave** — formed by the processes of coastal erosion (**abrasion, hydraulic action etc.** each of which should be explained) exploiting lines of weakness in the cliff face

★ **arch** — result of **erosion** on both sides of a headland

★ **stack** — result of **collapse** of roof of arch

★ **stump** — the result of continuing action of the sea

Coastal processes: marine erosion, transportation and deposition. You should understand terms of erosion, such as hydraulic action, abrasion, attrition, corrosion. You should use alternative words to demonstrate that you understand them, for example bumping and grinding for 'abrasion'. You should understand how material is transported in a coastal context, such as by longshore drift, and by wind action with the processes of saltation and suspension.

> You must be clear in the meaning of each of these terms and of how they operate in a coastal context.

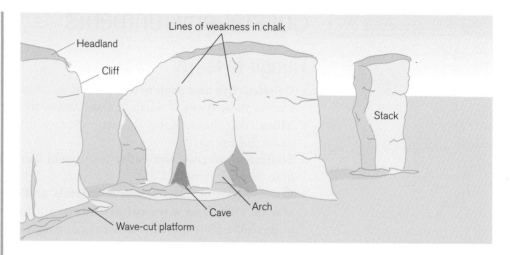

Figure 1.12 Coastal erosion

Coastal processes: land based sub-aerial weathering, mass movement and runoff. You should understand the various processes by which material is weathered on a coastline — frost shattering and biological forms of weathering. You should understand how materials can move on a coastline — rockfalls, landslides, mudflows and slumping. Runoff is also an important process during very wet weather.

Sea-level change: eustatic and isostatic change. You should understand the meaning of each of these terms and the factors that cause them to occur.

Impact of present and predicted sea-level increase. You should be aware of precise and located impacts, which may be located in any part of the world.

Coastal protection objectives and management strategies. You should be aware of the distinction between hard and soft engineering techniques in coastal management in general.

Hard engineering: sea walls, revetments, rip-rap, gabions, groynes and barrages. You should understand how each of these methods seeks to prevent coastal erosion in general.

Soft engineering: beach nourishment, dune regeneration, marsh creation, land use/activity management. You should understand how each of these methods seeks to prevent coastal erosion in general.

Key case studies

★ A case study of coastal erosion should be known in detail, with clear references to each of the physical and human causes of the event, and the social and economic impacts/consequences of that event. Events on a relatively small area of coastline will be easier to study. The area studied can be anywhere in the world, but there are well-documented case studies based on the east and south coasts of England.

★ A case study of coastal flooding should be known in detail, with clear references to each of the physical and human causes of the event, and the social and economic impacts/consequences of that event. Events on a relatively small area of coastline will be easier to study. The area studied can be anywhere in the world. Coastal flooding is often associated with weather events such as storms.

> ★ A case study of a hard engineering coastal management scheme should be known in detail. The issues relating to costs (disadvantages) and benefits (advantages) of the schemes should be investigated, including the potential for sustainable management.
>
> ★ A case study of a soft engineering coastal management scheme should be known in detail. The issues relating to costs (disadvantages) and benefits (advantages) of the schemes should be investigated, including the potential for sustainable management.
>
> For the hard and soft engineering management schemes, the costs/benefits can relate either to the area directly involved, or to other areas — for example, those further along the coastline, or nationally — and can be examined in terms of both their short-term and longer-term impacts.

Hint

1 Identify two or three features first, and then describe each by referring to shape, size, composition and relative position.

 ## Testing your knowledge and understanding

1 Study Figure 1.13. Describe the main physical features of the coastline shown.

➡ The **answers** to the **questions** are on pages 79–83

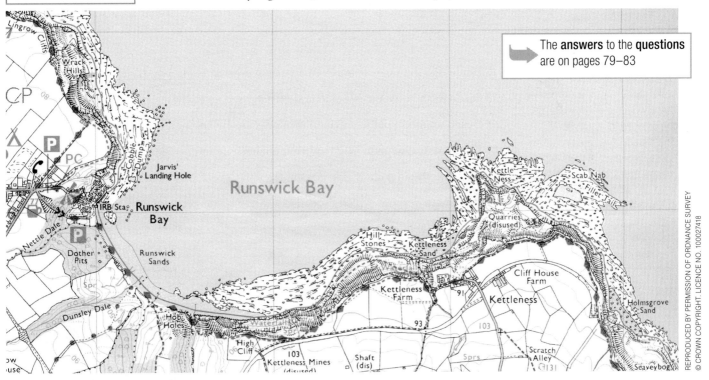

Figure 1.13

2 Choose *one* feature that you identified in answer to Question 1, and explain how it was formed.

3 Describe the characteristics of a sediment cell.

4 Give three differences between constructive and destructive waves.

5 Name the process that causes waves to appear to bend at a headland and become parallel to the coastline.

Hint

4 Make sure you give clear differences and use connective words such as 'whereas, on the other hand, however...'.

Hints

6 Although you can use terms to help you learn, when you write an answer you must show you understand what those terms mean. Use alternative verbs.

8 Note that there are two elements to this term — sub-aerial and weathering.

9 Note that there are two commands here — describe and explain. You must respond to both.

10 Note that there are two aspects of this question — describing location and then explaining it.

6 Outline four ways in which waves erode.

7 Explain the process of longshore drift.

8 Define the term 'sub-aerial weathering'.

9 Describe the characteristics of spits and explain their formation.

10 Study Figure 1.14. Describe and explain the contrasting locations of the beach landforms shown.

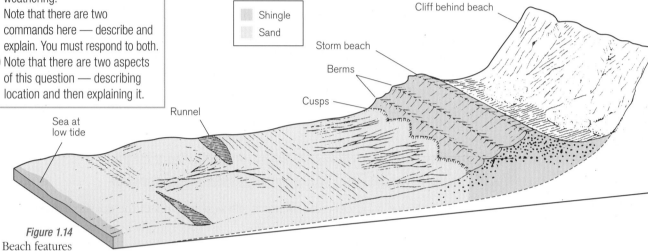

Figure 1.14
Beach features

Hints

12 To make the distinction clear, make sure that you use words that connect, e.g. 'whereas, on the other hand, however...'.

15 The impact on an area could be social, economic and environmental. You should refer to at least two of these.

17 To make the distinction clear, make sure that you use words that connect, e.g. 'whereas, on the other hand, however...'.

11 Briefly list the main features of a coastal erosion event you have studied.

12 Distinguish between isostatic and eustatic sea-level change.

13 Describe and explain one landform affected by submergence.

14 Describe and explain one landform created on an emergent coastline.

15 Describe the impact of one coastal flooding event you have studied.

16 Give three ways in which coastal flooding can be prevented or managed.

17 In the context of coastal protection, distinguish between hard engineering and soft engineering.

18 Study Figure 1.15 below. Explain how this coastline is being protected.

Hint

Make sure that you refer to features shown in the photograph in your response.

Figure 1.15

Hint

19 To make the distinction clear, make sure you use words that connect, e.g. 'whereas, on the other hand, however...'.

19 Distinguish between rip-rap and revetments.

20 Outline the term beach nourishment.

21 Give five main features of a soft engineering case study that you have studied.

22 Study Figure 1.16, a map of part of the Welsh coast. Describe the distribution of sand dunes and estuarine sands/salt marsh along this part of the coast.

Hint

Make good use of the place names and scale to help you describe the distributions.

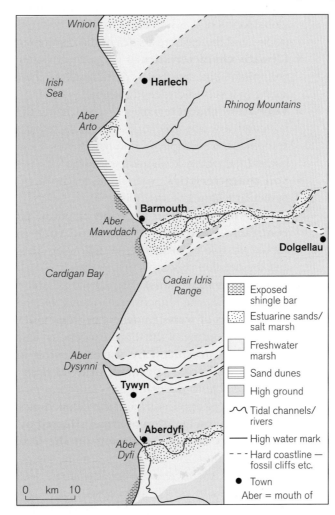

Figure 1.16 Map of part of the Welsh coast

23 Outline the sequence of coastal sand dune development.

24 Explain how salt marshes are created.

Hint

25 There are a number of processes involved here — be aware of the complexity of the task.

25 Explain why cliffs collapse.

26 Give three characteristics of a wave-cut platform.

27 Explain why some people suggest that there should be a 'do nothing' approach to coastal management.

28 What factors lead to the development of headlands and bays?

29 Explain why tides occur.

Hint

30 Note the command 'discuss'. You should provide two sides to this statement — for and against.

30 'Householders, faced with damage or destruction of their homes by coastal erosion or coastal flooding, should be compensated by the taxpayer.' Discuss this statement.

Hot desert environments and their margins

Things to learn

★ **The location of hot desert areas and their margins.** Apart from their exact global location, it is important to know where these areas are with respect to the tropics and the east/west sides of the continents.

★ **Climatic characteristics** — temperature patterns (particularly the diurnal range) and rainfall characteristics (particularly its intensity in relation to large amounts falling in a very short length of time)

★ **Vegetation characteristics** — particularly how plants are able to adapt to the hot desert climate. Categories should be recognised and known, i.e. ephemerals, xerophytes, phreatophytes and halophytes. Examples, such as the cactus, euphorbia and the tamarisk, should be known.

★ **Soil characteristics.** You should learn the general soil characteristics and the particular features of an aridisol.

★ **Landforms produced by wind erosion, particularly deflation hollows, ventifacts, yardangs, zeugen and rock pedestals.** For each feature you should be able to **describe** the following: shape, size (dimensions), orientation and the detailed processes that formed it.

★ **Sand dunes (barchans).** You should be able to **describe** sand dunes in terms of their shape, size (dimensions), orientation and the processes that shaped them.

★ **The sources of water in desert regions and the role of flooding.** You should know the meaning of the terms exogenous, endoreic and ephemeral.

★ **Landforms produced by water erosion and deposition: wadis, mesa/buttes, inselbergs, salt lakes, alluvial fans, pediments and badlands.** You should be able to **describe** each landform in terms of shape, size (dimensions), composition (if applicable) and the detailed processes that formed it.

★ **The names and location of areas affected by or at risk from desertification**

★ **The impact of desertification on the land and on people** — to include vegetation cover, the soil and its fertility, the development of dunes, increases in sand storms, the increase in treeless areas, declining agricultural production and the movement of people as a consequence

★ **Economic development within these regions** — such as management strategies for dealing with desertification, the fuelwood crisis, agricultural production and other economic sector development (e.g. mining, power generation and tourism)

Things to understand

In every physical section it is important that you understand the link between the shape/appearance of a landform and the processes that formed it. Taking the example of a **sand dune** (**barchan**), you should understand the following sequence:

★ migration of dunes caused by prevailing wind
★ horn-shaped, because the edges of the dune move faster as there is less sand
★ particles moved through saltation and surface creep
★ eddying beyond the dune crest allows a steep slope to be maintained

★ grain size on steep slopes maintains steepness with coarse grains avalanching downslope; gentler gradient at base with finer grains

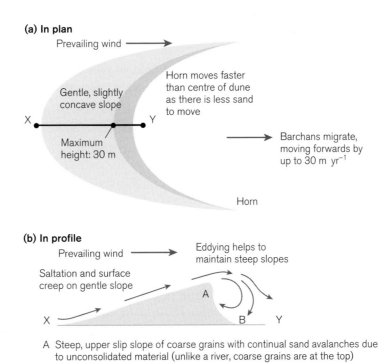

Figure 1.17 Barchans and their formation

The causes of aridity. You should understand what causes aridity in the places where it is the main feature of the climate. This should include the atmospheric circulation pattern, high-pressure systems in the tropics, wind patterns, continentality, the influence of relief and the position and effect of ocean currents.

The processes of mechanical weathering. You should understand how these processes work and the effect that they have on desert landscapes. Processes should include exfoliation, granular disintegration, shattering and block disintegration.

The processes of chemical weathering. You should understand how these processes work and the effect that they have on the desert landscape. Processes should include crystal growth, hydration and solution.

Processes of wind erosion. You should understand the processes of deflation and abrasion and how they affect desert landscapes.

Transportation of material by the wind. You should understand the ways in which the wind can transport material — suspension, saltation and surface creep.

The process of wind deposition. You should understand how the wind deposits material and how sand dunes (barchans) are therefore formed.

Flash flooding. You should understand why flash floods occur and the effect they can have on the desert landscape.

How water erosion and deposition are responsible for landscape features. You should understand the formation of wadis, mesa/buttes, inselbergs, salt lakes, alluvial fans, pediments, badlands.

The causes of desertification. You should understand:

★ the physical causes of desertification, which include the effects of lower rainfall and higher temperatures

★ the human causes, including the consequences of population growth, overcultivation, overgrazing and deforestation on the natural environment

The fuelwood crisis. You should understand why this crisis has occurred and what its role is in the process of desertification.

Key case studies

★ Desertification in the Sahel should be studied. This should cover the location, the desertification characteristics and causes (the weather pattern in recent years and its impact on the land and people and how people may have contributed), the fuelwood crisis, the impact of desertification (on water supply, food supply and people's livelihoods) and management/coping strategies.

★ The management of an area that contrasts with the Sahel should be studied. Suggestions are southwest USA, or southern Spain. You should consider and evaluate the strategies adopted with regard to land use and agriculture and the implications and potential for sustainability.

 ## Testing your knowledge and understanding

1 What do you understand by the term 'arid'?

Hint

2 From which two words is evapotranspiration formed?

2 What is evapotranspiration?

3 In which locations are hot deserts situated?

4 What is meant by the diurnal range of temperature? Why is it so large in hot desert areas?

Hints

5 Think of the conditions to which the plants need to be adapted — temperature, rainfall, sunshine etc.

7 Think of the atmospheric conditions that promote little rainfall, where you would find these, and how the global atmospheric system brings this about.

5 How are plants adapted to survive in hot desert areas?

6 What are the major differences between ephemerals and xerophytes?

7 How does the global atmospheric system contribute to the formation of hot deserts?

8 What other factors are responsible for bringing about the dry conditions of hot desert areas?

9 Study Figure 1.18, which shows the profile of an aridisol, a typical desert soil. Describe the process indicated by the arrow on the diagram.

10 Describe the major forms of mechanical weathering.

11 How does chemical weathering operate in desert areas?

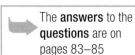

The **answers** to the **questions** are on pages 83–85

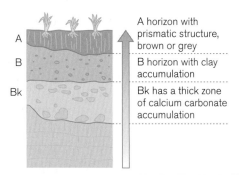

A horizon with prismatic structure, brown or grey

B horizon with clay accumulation

Bk has a thick zone of calcium carbonate accumulation

Figure 1.18 The profile of an aridisol

12 Describe the two forms of erosion that take place in desert areas.

13 What do you understand by the term 'reg'?

14 Figure 1.19 is a sketch of a rock pedestal, a typical product of wind erosion in deserts. Add labels to the sketch to show how the rock pedestal has been shaped.

Figure 1.19 A rock pedestal

Hint

15 Do wind and water behave in the same or a different way when transporting material?

Hint

19 What conditions promote rapid runoff? Think of the drainage basin hydrograph.

15 How does the wind transport material in hot desert areas?

16 Describe the formation of barchans (sand dunes).

17 What is an exogenous river?

18 What is a wadi?

19 Why are hot deserts subject to flash floods?

20 Study Figure 1.20, which is a photograph of a desert landscape. Explain how the features shown on the photograph were formed.

Figure 1.20 Monument Valley

21 Describe the formation of a bahada.

22 Describe the hot desert environment known as badlands.

23 What do you understand by the term 'desertification'?

24 How can climate change bring about desertification?

25 What are the human causes of desertification?

26 Where is the Sahel?

27 Give some of the suggested causes of desertification in the Sahel.

28 Describe some of the initiatives that have been attempted to try to alleviate the problem of desertification in the Sahel.

29 Figure 1.21 shows the visitor numbers to the Arches National Park, which is located on the semi-arid Colorado Plateau of southeast Utah (USA).
   a Describe the growth of visitor numbers as shown on Figure 1.21.
   b What would attract visitors to such a semi-arid area?

> **Hint**
>
> 29 For **a**, the best way to describe the increase is to look for breaks in the gradient. This will give you several segments which you can describe giving more detail. On Figure 1.21, there at least four identifiable breaks.

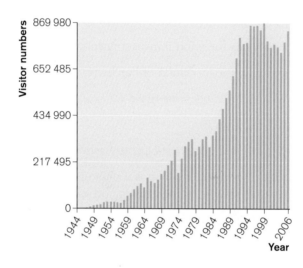

Figure 1.21 Arches National Park visitor numbers, 1947–2006

30 Why do some people want to retire to hot/semi-desert environments?

Topic **1.5**

Population change

Things to learn

★ **Population indicators.** For countries at different stages of development, you should know the vital rates (birth rate, death rate, fertility rate, infant mortality rate and how each of these changes over time; life expectancy; migration rate and population density). You should know the meaning of each term and the factors that affect it. You should be able to quote figures to illustrate how each term varies in countries at different stages of development.

★ **The demographic transition model (DTM).** You should know the diagram that makes up the DTM, and the various shapes of the population pyramids at each stage.

★ **The meaning, and causes, of migration**. Migration, either into an area, or from it, has a significant impact on the population of an area.

★ **Theories of the balance between population and resources.** The theories of Malthus and Boserup are well documented. You should learn one or both of these, or those of more recent geographers, such as Simon or Lomborg.

★ **Attempts to manage population change in two countries at different stages of development.** You should know in detail the ways in which the

> You should be aware of general factors that cause people to move to/from an area.

population change is being managed in each of these countries (see case studies below).

★ **Settlement case studies.** You should know the precise detailed characteristics of at least two of the following areas of study: an inner-city area, a suburban area, an area of rural–urban fringe and an area of rural settlement (see case studies on p.22).

Things to understand

Population change: the DTM, its validity and applicability in countries at different stages of development. You should understand the five stages of the DTM, their characteristics, and the factors that make them distinct. You should be able to debate whether or not the DTM is a useful model to use, particularly in relation to countries at different levels of development.

Population structures at different stages of the demographic transition. You should understand the meaning of the term population structure, and how it varies at each stage of the DTM. You should be able to identify countries that reflect the 'standard' shape of each stage of the DTM.

The impact of migration on population structure. You should understand how migration (both immigration and emigration) can impact on population structure.

The concept of the balance between population and resources should be studied, together with one or more theories of this interrelationship (e.g. Malthus, Boserup, Lomborg).

The implications of different structures for the balance between population and resources. You should understand how the population structure can affect the use of resources in a country.

Social, economic and political implications of population change. This is potentially a large topic, and it is important that you deconstruct the elements of it. First, population change can be either positive or negative; it can be due to natural change or migration, or both. Then, you have to think in terms of social, economic and political implications, each of which has a distinctive meaning. As this is such a broad topic, it is important that you refer to a range of examples in brief (breadth) rather than to case studies in detail (depth).

The spirit of this section is that the scale of study is national.

The way population change and migration affects the character of rural and urban areas. This continues the above theme to a more regional and local level. You should consider a range of rural and urban areas and the ways in which both natural population change (such as an ageing population) and migration influence the character of those areas. Again, as this is such a broad topic, it is important that you refer to a range of examples in brief (breadth), rather than to case studies in detail (depth).

Key case studies

★ Attempts to manage population change to achieve sustainable development with reference to case studies of countries at different stages of development should be covered. This covers a wide range of themes. The attempts could be to manage population change, or to manage resources (such as the Netherlands, or any of the Gulf States, such as Qatar). For management of population change, you could examine anti-natalist policies (such as in China, or Thailand) or pro-natalist policies (as in France and Russia). Make sure that you study two different case studies in detail that are taking place/have taken place in countries with a clear difference in terms of economic development.

★ Settlement case studies: two (or more) of the following areas should be compared: an inner-city area, a suburban area, an area of rural–urban fringe and an area of rural settlement. The case studies should include reference to characteristics such as housing, ethnicity, age structure, wealth and employment and the provision of services, and the implications of these for social welfare.

The basic requirement here is to consider two small-scale case studies, although you could study more. The case studies could all be based in the same urban area, but they do not need to be. You might want to use areas in different parts of the world, or UK, in order to highlight the differences between them. A useful starting point is the neighbourhood statistics website of the UK census (**www. neighbourhood.statistics.gov.uk**), where a postcode is required to enter the database. Details of each of the characteristics required above are given here, with the exception of services. You may have to use other sources of information such as fieldwork, or ICT-based sources of information such as Google Earth (Street View) and Yell.com to find this information. Having described your two (or more) chosen areas in detail, you must then consider how the characteristics impact on social welfare. This refers to the way in which people lead their lives in terms of education, housing, health, recreation and leisure, and employment. How and where do they access these facilities and services and what are the issues that arise?

Testing your knowledge and understanding

1 Distinguish between birth rate and fertility rate.

2 Why is infant mortality a good indicator of a country's development?

3 Study the table below.
 a Arrange the countries in order of development.
 b Suggest reasons for your chosen order.

Hint

1 To make the distinction clear, make sure that you use words that connect, e.g. 'whereas, on the other hand, however...'.

 The **answers** to the **questions** are on pages 85–90

Demographic variable	Country A	Country B	Country C	Country D
Crude birth rate/000	15	17	28	12
Crude death rate/000	6	7	8	11
Natural increase (%)	0.9	1	2	0.1
Infant mortality rate/000	31	15.6	66	5.7
Total fertility rate	1.8	2	3.3	1.7
% population aged under 15	23	26	40	19
% population aged over 65	7	6	3	16
Life expectancy at birth: male / *female*	69 / *71*	67 / *74*	59 / *59*	75 / *80*

Hint

4 You should consider more than one way in which this could occur.

Hints

For questions **5** and **6**, you are advised to illustrate your answer by referring to examples.

For question **7**, note that the question requires 'to what extent…'. You must make an overall statement in response to this.

4 How might the population density of an area change over time?

5 Explain how each of (a) tradition and (b) education influences birth rates.

6 Suggest how each of (a) economic development and (b) disease influences death rates.

7 Study the table below, which shows birth rates, death rates and growth rates for Thailand between 1950 and 2009. To what extent does Thailand fit the DTM for the time period shown?

Date	Birth rate (per 1000)	Death rate (per 1000)	Natural growth rate (%)
1960	45	14	3.1
1970	37	9	2.8
1980	28	7	2.1
1990	22	8	1.4
2000	17	8	0.9
2009	15	9	0.6

8 Describe how the population structure of a country in Stage 4 of the DTM is different from that of a country in Stage 2.

9 Give two reasons why some people believe the DTM is useful, and two reasons why some people believe it to be too limiting.

Hint

10 Note the double command here — you must complete two tasks.
When describing changes between population pyramids, refer to groups of people rather than to individual age groups.

10 Figure 1.22(a) shows the population pyramid for Poland in 2000. Figure 1.22(b) shows the population pyramid projected for 2050. Describe and suggest reasons for the changes between 2000 and 2050.

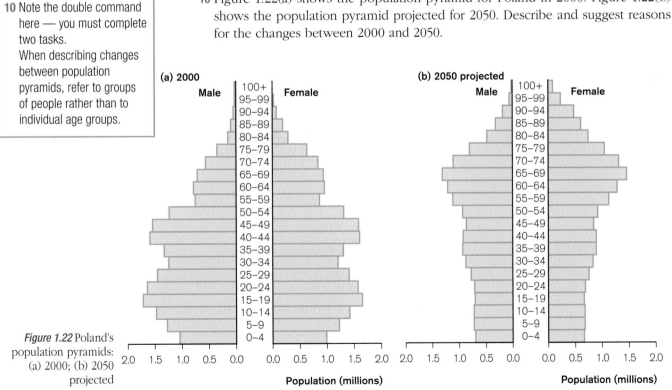

Figure 1.22 Poland's population pyramids: (a) 2000; (b) 2050 projected

11 Using examples, distinguish between forced and voluntary migration.

12 Study Figure 1.23. Describe the changes shown, and suggest two issues that could have arisen.

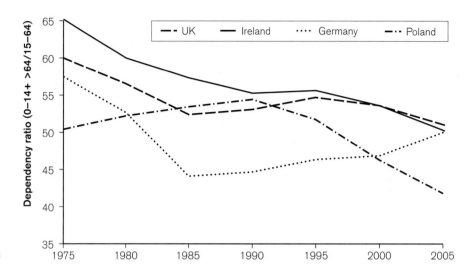

Figure 1.23 Dependency ratios

13 Outline two challenges that a youthful population presents for a country.

14 How does outward migration affect the population structure of an area?

15 Study Figure 1.24. Describe the possible migration into each of the two areas shown.

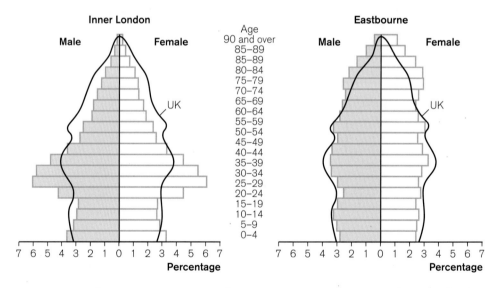

Figure 1.24 Migration

Hints

16 Note that the impacts should be only economic.
18 If you know only one such viewpoint, try to research another.

16 Summarise the economic impacts of in-migration on an area you have studied.

17 Define each of the terms 'overpopulation' and 'underpopulation'.

18 In the context of the balance between population and resources, summarise one optimistic viewpoint.

19 In 1996, the World Food Summit (WFS) set targets to eradicate hunger. The aim was to reduce the number of undernourished people in the world by 50% by 2015, compared with the 1990 level. Study Figure 1.25, which shows the situation in 2003. Describe the situation in 2003 and comment on the extent to which the data suggest that the situation has improved.

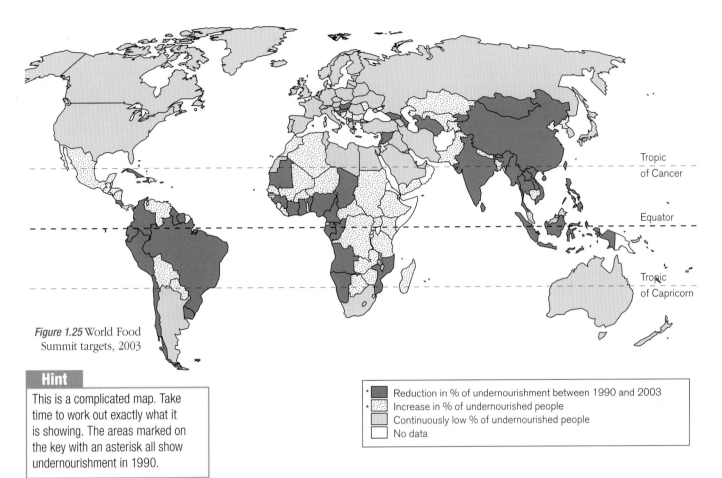

Figure 1.25 World Food Summit targets, 2003

* ▓ Reduction in % of undernourishment between 1990 and 2003
* ⋅ Increase in % of undernourished people
  Continuously low % of undernourished people
  No data

20 Describe the main features of a case study you have studied where population growth has been controlled.

21 Describe the main features of a case study you have studied where migration has been controlled.

22 Outline three consequences for a rural area in the UK where population is declining.

23 Outline three consequences for a rural area in the UK where population is growing.

24 For one small-scale area you have studied, describe how the population changes in the area have affected housing provision.

25 Give five contrasts (in terms of housing, ethnicity, age structure, wealth and employment) between two case studies you have undertaken of either: an inner-city area, a suburban area, an area of rural–urban fringe, an area of rural settlement.

26 Study Figures 1.26 (a) and (b). Describe the extent to which the distribution of the ethnic population has changed between 1981 and 2001.

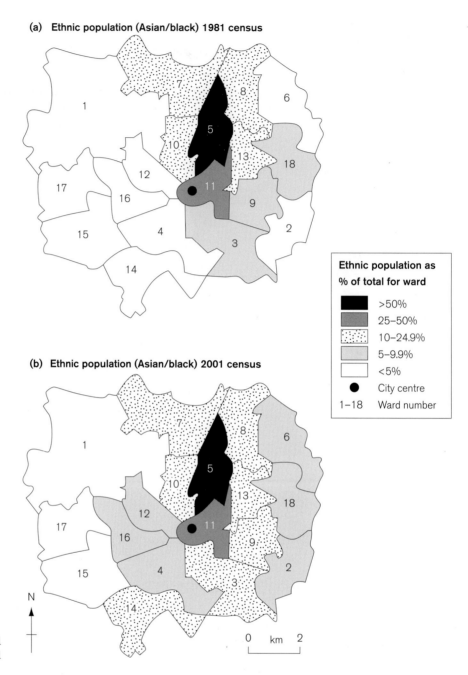

Figure 1.26 Ethnic population (a) 1981 (b) 2001

27 Outline how age structure and wealth may vary within a settlement.

28 Explain what is meant by the term 'social welfare'.

29 Suggest how employment rates in a settlement may impact on social welfare.

30 Outline and comment on the economic and political consequences of population change.

Hint

30 Note that population change can refer to losses and gains; and note the key words: economic and political. Be sure you know what these mean.

Figure 1.28

7 What do you understand by the term 'Green Revolution'?

8 What benefits have farmers received from the Green Revolution?

9 Are there any disadvantages to the farmer in using high-yielding varieties (HYV) of seeds?

10 What do you understand by the genetic modification (GM) of crops?

11 Why are some people very much against the use of GM crops?

12 Describe what is meant by integrated pest management.

13 What are growth hormones? Why has there been widespread opposition to their use in agriculture?

Hint

14 You have to initially ask 'appropriate to what?'

14 What do you understand by the term 'appropriate technology' when applied to agriculture?

15 Give an example of where appropriate technology has been a success in an agricultural area.

16 Give an example where land colonisation has increased agricultural production.

Hints

17 Land reform cannot really be about changing land use, so you have to concentrate on the ownership of land to find your answer.

19 In general usage, 'quota' refers to a share of something.

21 Look at the previous question.

17 What do you understand by the term 'land reform'?

18 What is the Common Agricultural Policy (CAP)?

19 Define the term 'quota' in terms of agricultural trade.

20 Under what circumstances do farmers receive subsidies?

21 Why have the farmers of the EU overproduced certain agricultural commodities in recent years?

22 What do you understand by 'set aside'?

23 What do you understand by the term 'environmental stewardship'?

24 In agricultural terms what is a buffer zone? What are the benefits of establishing them?

Hint

Do not describe the distribution by going around the chart and dealing with it segment by segment. Look for categories, largest/smallest, any surprises in the data.

25 Study Figure 1.29, which shows the carbon emissions associated with the transport of UK food. Comment on the information shown on the diagram.

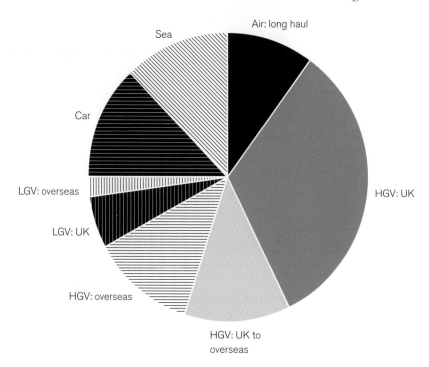

Figure 1.29 Carbon dioxide emissions associated with UK food transport, 2002

26 What is organic farming? Describe the growth of organic farming in the UK as shown on Figure 1.30.

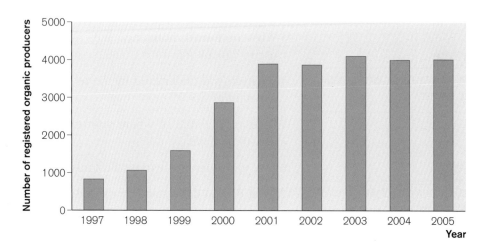

Figure 1.30 Registered organic producers in the UK, 1997–2005

27 What are the benefits to be had when food retailers sell an increasing amount of local produce?

28 What is an agribusiness?

29 Why are some people opposed to the increasing role of agribusinesses in the production, processing and distribution of food?

Hint

30 Think of a general definition of sustainability and then apply your answer to agriculture.

30 Define 'sustainability' in the context of food production.

Topic **1.7**

Energy issues

Things to learn

* ★ **Types of energy: renewable (flow) resources, non-renewable (stock) resources, primary/secondary energy.** You should be sure of the meaning of each of these terms, and the general factors that affect them.
* ★ **The primary energy mix considered in a national context.** The breakdown of energy production and consumption of one country should be studied and known.
* ★ **Global patterns of energy supply, consumption and trade; recent changes in these patterns.** The global pattern of each energy supply, consumption and trade should be studied together with how they have changed within the last 20–30 years.
* ★ **The environmental impact of energy production: fuelwood gathering; nuclear power and its management.** You should know the range of environmental impacts that energy production can have on the environment. You could also know other impacts, such as the possible link between energy production and global warming. You should support your knowledge of general impacts with reference to specific examples.
* ★ **The potential for sustainable energy supply and consumption: renewable energy — biomass, solar power, wind energy, wave energy and tidal energy; appropriate technology for sustainable development.** Be sure that you know the meaning of each of these terms, and the general factors that affect their development. It is much better if you can support any answer to a question on these systems with detailed exemplification of areas where they have been developed.
* ★ **Energy conservation: designing homes, workplaces and transport for sustainability.** There may be a temptation to be very generalised about this aspect of the unit. This approach is justifiable, but it will be enhanced with appropriate exemplification of where specific groups of homes, industry and transport have either been designed from scratch, or modified, to conserve energy and for sustainability. Good use of the internet, or, if possible, detail of examples local to you, should provide this.

> Try and get information that is as up to date as possible.

> A word of caution — it is advisable to use examples of where they have been adopted, rather than where they may be adopted.

Things to understand

The geopolitics of energy: conflict and cooperation in world affairs. You should be sure of the meaning of these terms and understand the factors that have caused there to be both conflict and cooperation in the context of energy supply and demand. The major feature here is the relationship between different countries/parts of the world in terms of their energy production and consumption, and with whom they trade (or do not trade) and why.

The use of fossil fuels: acid rain, the potential exhaustion of fossil fuels. You should understand the issues surrounding the causes and consequences of acid rain (also known as acid deposition) on the natural environment, buildings and people. You should also understand the potential impact of fossil fuels (coal, oil and natural gas) running out over the coming 30 years or so. You should consider how the use of fossil fuels could become more sustainable.

Consider both beneficial and adverse aspects of TNC operations, and try to access some good examples of where they occur.

The role of TNCs in world energy production and distribution. Many TNCs now wield great power. This has major consequences for many countries in the developing world and for investors in the developed world. The general principles of the ways in which TNCs operate should be understood fully and should then be related to at least one energy-based TNC.

Key case studies

★ One case study of the transfer of one energy source from area(s) of production to area(s) of consumption should be covered. This could be between countries, such as Russian gas to western Europe, or within a country such as the Trans-Alaskan pipeline.

★ One case study of one major energy-based TNC should be covered. The major petroleum based TNCs such as BP and Shell would be good examples to use, although new emerging TNCs such as Gazprom would also be interesting.

Case studies at national scale of two contrasting approaches to managing energy supply and demand should be covered. You may not need to carry out new studies to cover this section of the specification as you may have already studied a number of approaches to energy production. However, you should ensure that you get a contrast at a *national* scale. One investigation could be to study an approach that increases production to meet demand, such as the use of nuclear power in France, and compare this with an approach that seeks to limit energy consumption, such as conservation schemes in some developed countries, for example Sweden and Finland.

Testing your knowledge and understanding

Hints

1 To make the distinction clear, make sure that you use words that connect, e.g. 'whereas, on the other hand, however...'.

3 To describe a change you must have some idea of what the situation was at some point in time, so that you can then describe increases and decreases.

4 The command 'comment' means you have to write something that can be inferred from the data, or arises from the data.

1 Distinguish between flow resources and stock resources.

2 What is the difference between primary and secondary energy?

3 How has the UK's primary energy mix changed over the last 20 years?

4 Study Figure 1.31. Comment on the trends in world energy consumption.

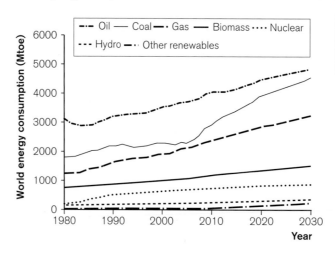

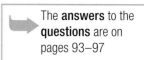

The **answers** to the **questions** are on pages 93–97

Figure 1.31 World energy consumption projection by fuel (million tonnes oil equivalent)

Hint

5 When describing global patterns, refer to regions or groups of countries.

5 Describe the global patterns of energy supply.

6 Study Figure 1.32. Comment on the global pattern of energy consumption.

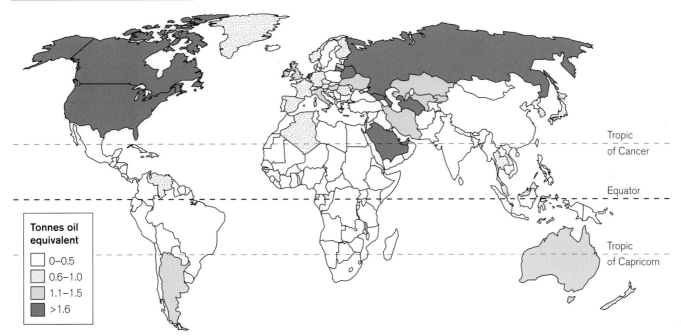

Tonnes oil equivalent

- ☐ 0–0.5
- ▨ 0.6–1.0
- ▨ 1.1–1.5
- ▉ >1.6

Figure 1.32 World energy consumption per capita, 2007

Hint

6 The command 'comment' means you have to write something that can be inferred from the data, or arises from the data.

7 Study Figure 1.33, which shows the major trade movements in oil in 2007. Describe the pattern of trade shown.

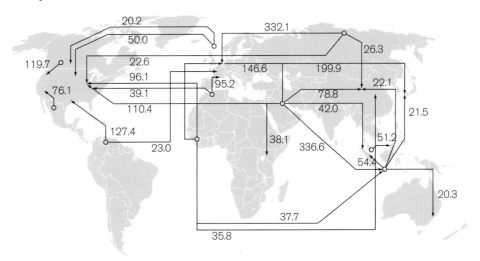

Figure 1.33 Major trade movements in oil, 2007 (million tonnes)

Hint

9 Note the question requires 'to what extent'. You must make an overall statement in response to this.

8 State what OPEC stands for and outline their main aims.

9 To what extent is the global supply of energy dependent on cooperation between countries?

10 How is natural gas transported between the main producers and consumers?

11 Describe and explain the impact of the use of fossil fuels on the environment.

12 State which type of location is best suited to produce:
- **a** solar energy
- **b** wind power

Hint

13 Note the question requires 'to what extent'. You must make an overall statement in response to this.

Hint

15 The command 'comment' means you have to write something that can be inferred from the data, or arises from the data.

13 To what extent do TNCs control the production and distribution of oil?

14 Give three reasons why coal has declined in importance as a major source of energy in the UK?

15 Study Figure 1.34. Comment on the projected changes in the UK's generation of electricity by gas-fired and nuclear power stations.

(a) UK gas sources

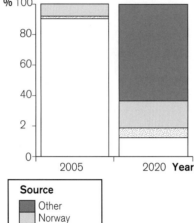

Source
- Other
- Norway
- Europe
- UK produced

- Nuclear power provided 22% of UK electricity in 2005. This is expected to fall to under 10% by 2020.
- Gas provided 40% of UK electricity in 2005, this is expected to rise to over 60% by 2020.

(b) Decommissioning of UK nuclear power stations

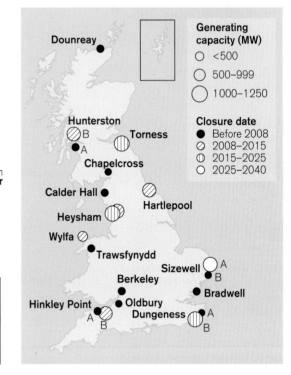

Figure 1.34 Changes in the UK's generation of electricity by gas-fired and nuclear power stations, 2005–40

16 Outline the environmental problems linked to fuelwood gathering in developing countries.

17 Describe ways in which biomass can be used to harness energy.

18 Outline the main arguments in favour of the development of nuclear power.

19 Distinguish between wave and tidal power.

20 Study Figure 1.35. Describe and comment on the trends shown.

Hints

18 Note that question only requires statements in favour of nuclear power — many people tend to focus on the negative aspects.
19 To make the distinction clear, make sure that you use words that connect, e.g. 'whereas, on the other hand, however...'.

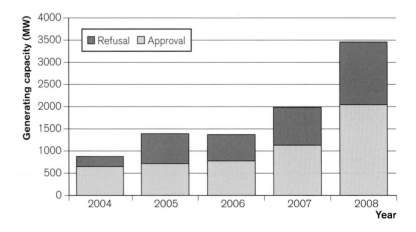

Figure 1.35 Planning approvals and refusals for wind farms in the UK, 2004–08

Hint

21 A question such as this is best answered with brief references to supportive case studies.

21 What types of energy might be most appropriate for development in developing countries?

22 Outline one global agreement designed to combat the environmental damage related to unsustainable energy use.

23 Study Figure 1.36. In what ways can energy be conserved in the home?

Hint

The key here is to use the figure and the labels on it as a stimulus. Do not just repeat the labels — do something extra with them.

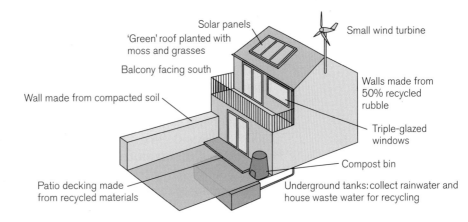

Figure 1.36 Energy conservation

24 What steps can be taken by businesses and workplaces to ensure that they conserve energy?

25 Outline how transport policies have been designed for sustainability.

Hint

25 A question such as this is best answered with brief references to supportive case studies.

26 Discuss the problems associated with the management of nuclear power.

27 Explain why some people say that it is likely that supplies of oil will become exhausted.

Hint

28 The command 'comment' means you have to write something that can be inferred from the data, or arises from the data.

28 Study Figure 1.37, which gives details of the largest petroleum TNCs. Comment on the information shown.

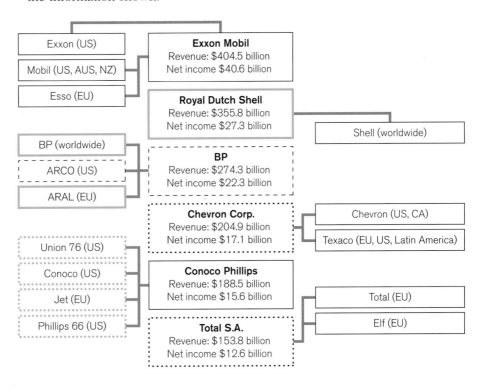

Figure 1.37 Petroleum TNCs

Hint

30 The command 'discuss' requires you to present an argument that is balanced.

29 Describe two contrasting approaches of managing energy supply at a national scale.

30 Discuss advantages and disadvantages of two contrasting approaches to managing energy.

Topic **1.8**

Health issues

Things to learn

★ **Global patterns of health, morbidity and mortality.** You should know the meaning of each of these terms, and the general factors that affect them. The global patterns of various aspects of mortality (for example, death rates and infant mortality rates) and some aspects of morbidity, e.g. influenza, should be studied.

★ **Food and health: malnutrition, periodic famine, obesity.** You should know the meaning of each of these terms, and the general factors that cause them. You should be aware of the general consequences of each, although in each case it is better if you can support these with detailed knowledge of an area where they are prevalent.

★ **Health matters in a globalising world economy: TNCs and pharmaceutical research, production and distribution; tobacco transnationals.** You should know examples of each of these types of TNC, and where they operate in the world.

Morbidity can refer to any aspect of illness, and so you should be aware of more than one kind of illness.

Things to understand

Health in world affairs. You should be aware of the general importance of health in global, national and local areas.

Contrasting healthcare approaches in countries at different stages of development. It is important that at least two national healthcare systems are examined — their main characteristics, with named examples of where they operate. The two countries must have contrasting levels of economic development — choose at least one from the developed world and at least one from the developing world.

How do aspects of poor health impact on how people live their lives?

Health matters in a globalising world economy: TNCs and pharmaceutical research, production and distribution; tobacco transnationals. In addition to understanding the roles of the two identified types of TNC, the general principles of the ways in which TNCs operate should be fully understood. You should consider both beneficial and adverse aspects of their operations.

Regional variations in health and morbidity in the UK: factors affecting these regional variations — age structure, income and occupation type, education, environment and pollution. Variations in health within the UK are regularly featured on television and in other media outlets. On each occasion, some attempt at explanation is made — monitor these reports and collect the information. The essential aspect here is that variations are described, both between and within regions, with some attempt at explanation in terms of socioeconomic factors, behaviours or the environment.

This area of research is still developing, and hence any reasonable view or opinion will be accepted.

Key case studies

★ One infectious disease (e.g. malaria, HIV/AIDS) its global distribution and its impact on health, economic development and lifestyle should be studied. Two examples are given in the specification, but you could choose to study another, such as cholera. Whichever disease you choose, make sure that it is infectious and has a global distribution (areas where it tends to occur, and not occur). There is also the requirement to study the impact of each disease on the health of the population, the level of economic development of the area where it is prevalent and the lifestyle of the people. It is also a good idea to examine ways in which the disease can be managed and/or prevented.

★ One non-communicable disease ('disease of affluence') (e.g. coronary disease, cancer) its global distribution and its impact on health, economic development and lifestyle should be studied. Two examples are given in the specification, but you could choose to study a variation of one of these, e.g. lung cancer only. Whichever disease you choose, make sure that it is non-communicable and has a global distribution (areas where it tends to occur, and not occur). There is also the requirement to study the impact of each disease on the health of the population, the level of economic development of the area where it is prevalent and the lifestyle of the people. It is also a good idea to examine ways in which the disease can be managed and/or prevented.

★ Malnutrition, periodic famine and obesity are included in the specification. A case study of the causes, effects and possible solutions of famine (which may result in malnutrition) could be studied. You should be aware of the causes, and consequences, of obesity in an area of study such as the UK or the USA.

★ Age, gender, wealth and their influence on access to facilities for exercise, healthcare, and good nutrition are included in the specification. This can be best examined by means of a research investigation, which may include fieldwork, within a small-scale area (for example an electoral ward). Using data from the census you could compare the demographic and social make-up of a population with the health-related facilities available. Be sure to evaluate the work you do — is the level, or provision, of health-related activity appropriate or not?

★ A local case study on the implications of the above for the provision of healthcare systems is a requirement of the specification. This could extend the above investigation into the provision of healthcare systems in a local area. It would be advisable to look at a slightly larger area, such as a Primary Care Trust (PCT) as most facilities such as A&E, maternity and mental health are organised at this scale. The NHS publishes detailed health profiles for each area covered by a PCT. You can access this information at **www.healthprofiles.info.**

Hint

1 To make the distinction clear, make sure that you use words that connect, e.g. 'whereas, on the other hand, however...'.

Testing your knowledge and understanding

1 Distinquish between morbidity and mortality.

2 Define the term 'maternal mortality'.

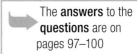
The **answers** to the **questions** are on pages 97–100

3 Describe the global distribution of one non-communicable disease ('disease of affluence') you have studied.

4 Study Figure 1.38. Describe the global distribution of cholera as shown on the map.

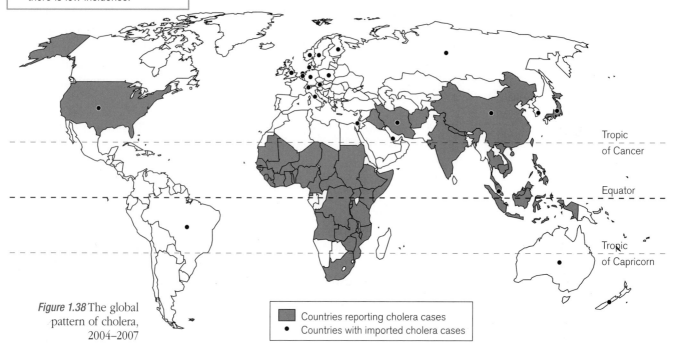

Figure 1.38 The global pattern of cholera, 2004–2007

Tropic of Cancer

Equator

Tropic of Capricorn

☐ Countries reporting cholera cases
● Countries with imported cholera cases

5 Outline the impact that an infectious disease can have on the lifestyle of the people affected.

6 Give three ways in which an infectious disease can be prevented or managed.

7 Study Figure 1.39. Comment on the trends shown.

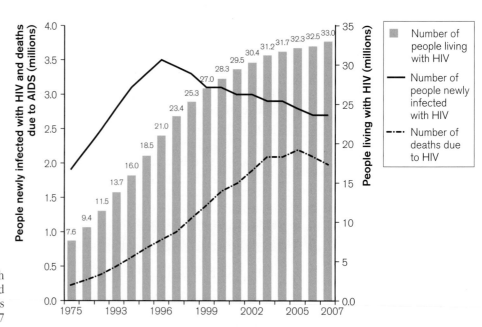

Figure 1.39 Number of people living with HIV, number of people newly infected with HIV and number of AIDS deaths in the world (millions), 1990–2007

■ Number of people living with HIV

— Number of people newly infected with HIV

–·– Number of deaths due to HIV

8 Assess the economic impact of one non-communicable disease ('disease of affluence')

9 Outline the impact of one non-communicable disease ('disease of affluence') on health.

10 Distinguish between malnutrition and undernourishment.

11 Explain two physical causes of periodic famine.

12 Explain two human causes of periodic famine.

13 With reference to one example, outline the effects of famine on the people affected.

14 State ways in which famine can be prevented in the long term.

15 Study Figure 1.40. Describe the information shown.

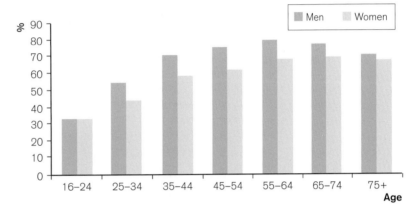

Figure 1.40 Percentage of adults who are overweight including obese, by age and gender, England, 2007

16 Discuss the impact of obesity on people's health and the strategies adopted to address it.

17 Summarise the main features of a National Health Service such as that in the UK or Canada.

18 Study Figure 1.41. Comment on the information given in it.

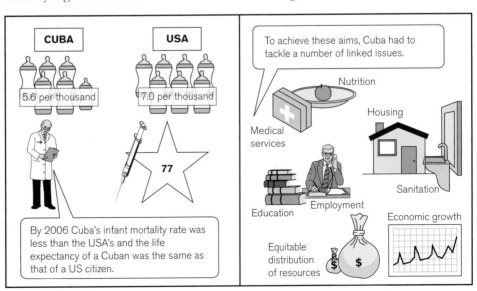

Figure 1.41 Cuba and USA comparison

19 Comment on the contrasting healthcare approaches in two countries at different stages of development.

20 Discuss issues associated with pharmaceutical TNCs and their products.

21 Pharmaceutical TNCs are often criticised for the profits they make. Outline why the TNCs say these profits are necessary.

22 Outline ways in which tobacco TNCs are impacting on the lives of people in the developing world.

23 Study Figure 1.42 relating to tobacco control policies in 194 countries. Comment on the information shown.

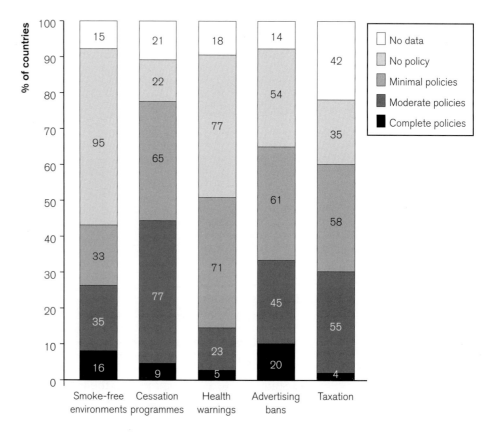

Numbers in columns show number of countries. Note that for taxation, 'No policy' implies an excise tax rate 25% or less. For smoke-free environments, 'No policy' means no smoke-free legislation or no smoke-free legislation covering either healthcare or educational facilities.

Figure 1.42 Tobacco control policies

24 Describe and suggest reasons for regional variations in morbidity within the UK.

25 Define the term 'Primary Care Trust' (PCT).

26 Briefly describe the provision of healthcare in your local area.

27 Identify two charitable organisations that play an important role in healthcare provision.

28 Study Figure 1.43, which shows a part of the Health Profile for two PCTs in England. Describe and comment on the differences between the two areas.

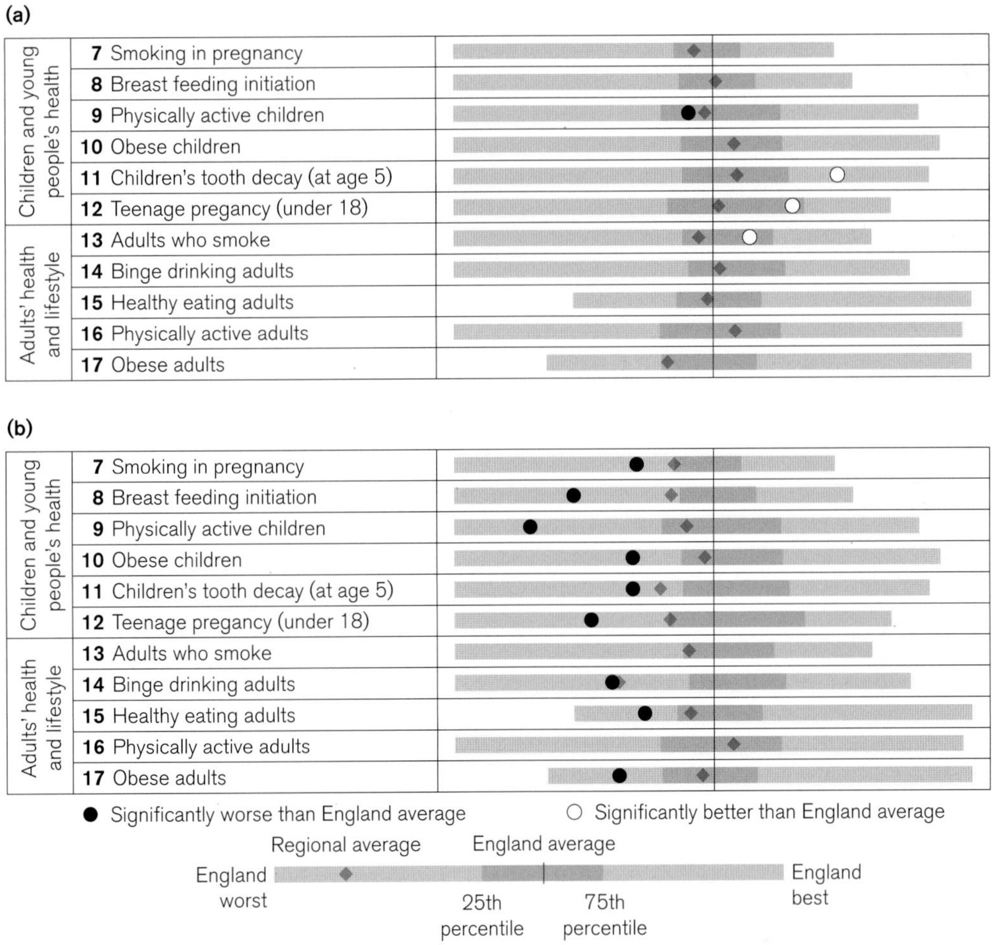

Figure 1.43 Part of the Health Profile for a PCT in (a) eastern England; and (b) northern England

(a)

Children and young people's health	**7** Smoking in pregnancy			
	8 Breast feeding initiation			
	9 Physically active children			
	10 Obese children			
	11 Children's tooth decay (at age 5)			
	12 Teenage pregancy (under 18)			
Adults' health and lifestyle	**13** Adults who smoke			
	14 Binge drinking adults			
	15 Healthy eating adults			
	16 Physically active adults			
	17 Obese adults			

(b)

Children and young people's health	**7** Smoking in pregnancy			
	8 Breast feeding initiation			
	9 Physically active children			
	10 Obese children			
	11 Children's tooth decay (at age 5)			
	12 Teenage pregancy (under 18)			
Adults' health and lifestyle	**13** Adults who smoke			
	14 Binge drinking adults			
	15 Healthy eating adults			
	16 Physically active adults			
	17 Obese adults			

● Significantly worse than England average   ○ Significantly better than England average

Regional average   England average

England worst   25th percentile   75th percentile   England best

Hint

29 The specification requires you to examine the influence of age, gender and wealth on access to healthcare. Here you must focus on one of these, and be precise.

29 With reference to an example, explain how gender can influence access to local healthcare systems.

30 With reference to a local case study, assess the relative importance of age, gender, wealth on the provision of healthcare, exercise and good nutrition.

UNIT 3

Contemporary geographical issues

Plate tectonics and associated hazards

Things to learn

★ **The structure of the Earth.** You should know the meaning of the following terms: core, crust (continental and oceanic), mantle, lithosphere, asthenosphere. You should know about thermal convection currents operating within the asthenosphere and sea-floor spreading.

★ **Features of constructive (divergent) margins.** You should be able to **describe** and know the formation of oceanic ridges, submarine volcanic activity and rift valleys.

★ **Features of destructive (convergent) margins.** You should be able to know what is happening at oceanic/continental convergence, oceanic/oceanic convergence and continental/continental convergence. You should be able to **describe** and know the formation of the following features: ocean trenches, fold mountains, island arcs, explosive volcanic activity.

★ **Conservative margins**

★ **Hot spots**

★ **The distribution of volcanic activity**

★ **Intrusive volcanic landforms** — to include batholiths, dykes, sills and metamorphic aureoles

★ **Extrusive volcanic landforms** — to include the main forms of lava: basaltic, andesitic and rhyolitic. Features to include: lava plateaux, basic/shield volcanoes, acid/dome volcanoes, ash and cinder cones, composite cones and calderas

★ **Minor volcanic forms** — to include solfatera, geysers, hot springs/boiling mud

★ **The impact of volcanic activity.** You should be able to differentiate between primary effects (tephra, pyroclastic flows, lava flows, volcanic gases) and secondary effects (lahars, flooding, tsunamis, volcanic landslides, climate change).

★ **The focus and epicentre of earthquakes**

★ **Distribution of earthquakes**

★ **Magnitude and frequency of earthquakes**

★ **Impact of earthquakes.** You should be able to differentiate between the primary effect of ground shaking and the secondary effects of soil liquefaction, landslides/ avalanches, effects on people and the built environment.

★ **The nature and effects of tsunamis**

Things to understand

The theory of plate tectonics. You should understand how this theory developed and the evidence that supports its development.

Palaeomagnetism and sea-floor spreading. You should understand how magnetic striping occurs, the importance of this palaeomagnetic evidence and how this indicates the process of sea-floor spreading.

The process of subduction. You should understand how this process occurs and the effects it has on the edges of both continental and oceanic plates.

Vulcanicity. It is important to understand both the causes and nature of volcanic activity.

Managing volcanic activity. You should understand how people and authorities are able to manage volcanic activity. This could come about through your case studies (see below) as response to an event is a detailed part of your investigation.

Causes of earthquakes. You should understand what causes an earthquake and how seismic waves travelling through the Earth give information on the internal structure of the planet.

Measurement of earthquakes. You should understand how earthquakes are measured both in terms of the instrument used and the scales on which they are recorded (Richter, Mercalli).

Causes of tsunamis. You should understand how such waves are generated.

Managing earthquake activity. As with volcanic activity you should understand how people and authorities are able to manage earthquake activity. This can come through case studies.

Key case studies

★ You are required to make two case studies of recent **volcanic events**. In this instance, 'recent' means ideally within the last 30 years. The two events should be taken from contrasting areas of the world. The best solution to these instructions is to choose one from a developing country and one from a developed area. In this way you can best bring out the differences in impact and the way in which the people/authorities coped with volcanic events. In each case the following should be examined:
  – the nature of the volcanic hazard, i.e. the way in which the eruption took place
  – the impact of the event
  – how people and the authorities (local and external) responded to the hazard

★ You are also required to make two case studies of recent **seismic events**, i.e. earthquakes. In this instance, 'recent' means ideally within the last 30 years. The instructions are exactly the same as those for the volcanic events above. In each case, though, the following should be examined:
  – the nature of the seismic hazard, i.e. the strength of the earthquakes and any particular features of it such as depth, ground acceleration, etc.
  – the impact of the event
  – the preparation within the area, and how people and authorities (local and external) responded to the event

★ Good examples of events on which you could base your case studies include:

★ **Volcanic activity**: Montserrat (1995–96), Mt Etna (1991–93) and Nyiragongo (2002)

★ **Earthquakes**: Kobe (1995), Gujurat (2001), Sumatra (2004), Kashmir (2005) and Sichuan (China) (2008)

Such events happen frequently and so it is important to keep up with the information. Case studies in textbooks and other publications are the best the authors can find for you up to the time of printing. As geography students, it is important to search out new events and use the information that you have collected in the examinations. Examiners will always credit at a high level, in this context, students who make attempts to keep their work as up to date as possible.

In recent times, there were two large earthquakes that were well documented — those in Haiti and Chile (early 2010). Try to find as much information as you can about these events and their impact on the peoples of both countries. Do the same for any volcanic or earthquake events that occur after the publication of this book.

Testing your knowledge and understanding

1 Explain the terms 'lithosphere' and 'asthenosphere'.

2 What are the differences between oceanic and continental plates?

3 When Alfred Wegener published his theory of continental drift, how did he describe the distribution of land and ocean? Why did his theories fail to gain any real acceptance before the 1950s?

4 What was the original geological and biological evidence that Alfred Wegener used in his attempt to show that the continents had drifted apart?

5 What is sea-floor spreading?

6 How does the study of palaeomagnetism give evidence for sea-floor spreading?

7 Transform faults are associated with sea-floor spreading. How are transform faults created?

8 Study Figure 3.1 which shows what happens in continental areas when plates move apart. Complete the diagram by adding labels to show what is taking place.

Figure 3.1 Cross-section of a rift valley

9 Explain the process of subduction.

10 Study Figure 3.2 which shows what happens when an oceanic plate meets a continental plate at a point of convergence. Complete the diagram by adding labels to show what is taking place.

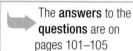

Hints

2 Think of age, density, thickness and composition.
3 With regard to the non-acceptance of his theory, concentrate on the name of the theory, i.e. continental drift.

The **answers** to the **questions** are on pages 101–105

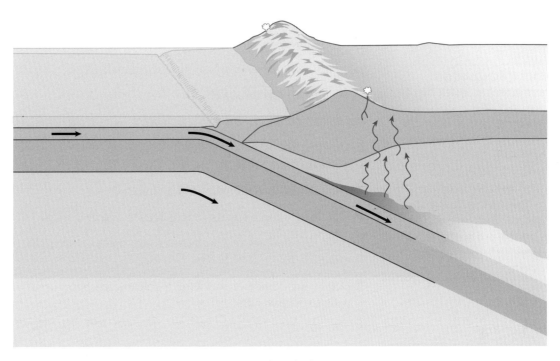

Figure 3.2 Cross-section of oceanic/continental plate convergence at a destructive plate margin

Hints

11 As the plates are likely to be very similar, will subduction be an issue?

14 Think of the causes of volcanic action. Where is this likely to happen?

11 What happens when two continental plates meet?

12 What happens on conservative margins?

13 How do hot spots form?

14 Describe the distribution of volcanic activity on a global scale.

15 Describe the appearance and formation of shield volcanoes.

16 Figure 3.3 shows a cross-section of a composite volcano. Add labels to describe the main features of the volcano and what happens during an eruption.

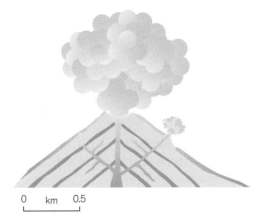

0   km   0.5

Figure 3.3 A composite volcano

Hint

18 When volcanoes erupt, they first eject various types of material.

17 Describe the minor features that volcanic activity can produce.

18 What are the primary effects of a volcanic event?

19 What is a lahar?

20 How can tsunamis be generated by volcanic eruptions?

21 What causes an earthquake?

22 What information do seismic waves give us that helps in an understanding of the Earth's interior?

23 Explain the global distribution of earthquakes.

24 What is the Richter scale?

25 Explain the process of soil liquefaction.

26 Describe the effects that earthquakes may have upon people and on the built environment.

27 What determines the impact of a tsunami?

28 How have people sought to manage the volcanic hazard through prediction?

29 How can people and authorities attempt to lessen the impact of earthquake events?

30 Does your chance of surviving a volcanic eruption or an earthquake depend on your level of wealth?

Hints

23 Think of the causes of earthquakes and where they are likely to occur.

29 As with all hazards, in terms of lessening the impact you should be thinking in terms of prediction, prevention and protection.

30 What will having money do for your chances of protecting yourself? Don't forget that being a member of a wealthy society (in relative terms) is equally important, i.e. collective wealth.

Topic **3.2**

Weather and climate and associated hazards

Things to learn

* ★ **The structure of the atmosphere.** You should know the composition of the atmosphere and know the meaning of the following terms: troposphere, tropopause, stratosphere and stratopause.
* ★ **The atmospheric heat budget**
* ★ **The general atmospheric circulation.** You should know the pattern of planetary surface winds and pressure systems, and particularly the importance of the pressure gradient. You should know about the following systems: Hadley cells, inter-tropical convergence zone (ITCZ), the trade winds, Ferrel cells, polar cells.
* ★ **The upper atmospheric circulation** — including knowledge of the following: polar-front jet stream, subtropical jet stream, Rossby waves
* ★ **Oceanic circulation**
* ★ **The basic characteristics of the climate of the British Isles, i.e. the cool temperate western maritime (CTWM).** You should know details of temperature, precipitation and winds.
* ★ **Air masses affecting the British Isles** — to include arctic, polar maritime, polar continental, tropical maritime, tropical continental
* ★ **The origin and nature of depressions.** You should know the meaning of the following terms: warm front, cold front, warm sector. You should also be able to recognise a depression on a synoptic chart.
* ★ **The sequence of weather associated with a depression**
* ★ **The origin and nature of anticyclones and the weather associated with them, including the formation of radiation fog.** You must be able to recognise a high-pressure system (anticyclone) on a synoptic chart.
* ★ **Storm events in the British Isles**

* **The basic characteristics of one of the following climates: tropical wet and dry, tropical monsoon or equatorial.** You are only required to study one of these climates.
* **Tropical revolving storms (hurricanes/typhoons/cyclones)**. The main characteristics that you should know are distribution, magnitude and frequency, prediction and impact.
* **The urban heat island effect**
* **Other features of urban climate** — to include precipitation, fog and thunderstorms
* **The air quality of urban areas and policies aimed at reducing pollution.** You should know the meaning of the following: particulate pollution and photochemical smog.
* **Urban winds**
* **Evidence for climatic change over the last 20000 years.** You should know about the following: pollen analysis, dendrochronology, ice-core analysis, sea-floor analysis, radiocarbon dating, Coleoptera, changing sea levels, glacial deposits and historical records.
* **Recent evidence for global warming**
* **The effects of global warming.** You should be able to deal with the following: rising sea levels, climatic change, extreme events and their effect on the climate of the British Isles and your chosen tropical climate.
* **International and national responses to global warming** — to include clean air legislation, reduction of greenhouse gas emissions, carbon credits, the Rio Earth Summit and the Kyoto conference; local responses could include home insulation, recycling, increasing use of public transport and increased home efficiency.

> As this is an ongoing topic, you should keep your material up to date. In particular, you should have information on the Copenhagen conference in 2009 and its outcome.

Things to understand

Climatic controls. You should understand how climate is influenced by the following: the atmospheric heat budget, the general circulation of the atmosphere (including surface planetary winds, atmospheric pressure and the upper atmospheric circulation), oceanic circulation, latitude and altitude.

The effect of air masses on the climate of the British Isles. You should understand how air masses change (or reinforce) their characteristics as they move towards the British Isles and how this affects our weather. You should also understand how the differences between winter and summer come about.

The weather associated with the passage of a depression. You should be able to relate the weather to the passage of the warm front, the warm sector, passage of the cold front and the weather behind that front.

The weather associated with an anticyclone. You should understand why the weather in an anticyclone is different in winter from that in summer.

Fog formation. You should understand how fog forms, particularly radiation fog.

Storm events in the British Isles. You should understand how such events are formed and how they impact on the region (see case studies overleaf).

Climate in the chosen tropical region. You should be able to explain this climate. In particular, you should be able to explain the role of subtropical anticyclones and the ITCZ.

Tropical revolving storms. You must be able to explain how such storms are generated and understand the conditions under which this happens.

Urban climate. You should understand why temperature, precipitation (thunderstorms and fogs), winds and air quality vary between the urban area and its surroundings and within the urban area.

> You must look at policies in at least two different cities.

Pollution reduction policies. You should understand how the problem of poor air quality is being tackled.

Climatic change. You should understand how the methods listed above (pollen analysis etc.) provide evidence of climatic change in the last 20 000 years.

The causes of global warming. You should understand the arguments with regard to global warming that are taking place at the present time.

> You should try to understand the effectiveness of newly introduced policies and climate summits, such as that held in Copenhagen in 2009.

The predicted effects of global warming on the climate of the British Isles and the chosen tropical region.

The effectiveness of strategies employed to currently reduce the impacts of global warming. In particular, you should understand the reasoning behind the 'think globally, act locally' approach.

Key case studies

★ You need to know in detail one case study of a significant storm event that has affected the British Isles in the last 30 years. You must make specific reference to the weather conditions experienced and the impacts and consequences of this event. The short- and long-term responses to the storm should also be considered. The great storm affecting the south of England in 1987 would be a good example for the case study.

★ You need to make a study of *two* contrasting tropical revolving storm events. In the case study, you should look at the geography of the area, the storm tracks, the impacts and the responses to each event. A good contrast would be to take one storm that affected a developed country (such as USA or Australia) and another which affected a much poorer area (such as Nicaragua or Myanmar (Burma)).

Testing your knowledge and understanding

1 Describe the structure of the atmosphere.

Hint

2 The heat must go somewhere!

2 If low latitudes receive more solar energy than they lose to space, why are these regions not becoming hotter through time?

> The **answers** to the **questions** are on pages 105–110

3 What are Hadley cells?

Hint

Ocean currents are classified as either hot or cold. What do ocean currents take from the areas from which they flow? Think of the Gulf Stream/North Atlantic Drift.

4 Figure 3.4 shows the world's oceanic circulation. How does this pattern of water flow affect the climate of continental areas?

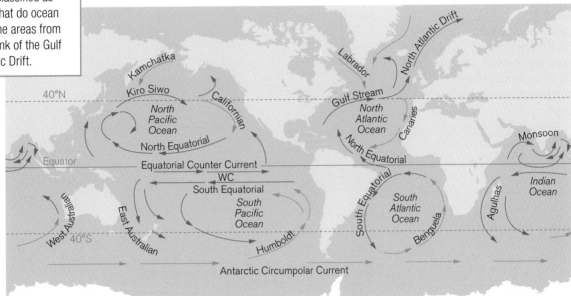

Figure 3.4 Oceanic circulation

5 How does latitude affect climate?

6 Study Figure 3.5, which shows the effect of melting Arctic ice on water movement in the North Atlantic. If this happens, what will be the effect on the climate of the British Isles?

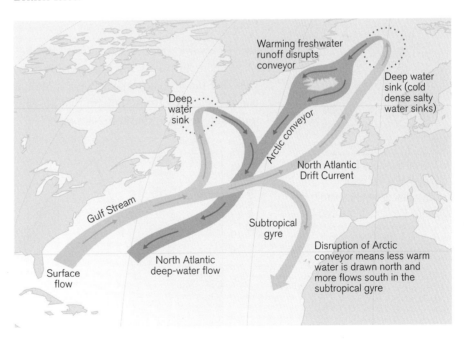

Figure 3.5 Effect of melting Arctic ice on ocean currents

7 Figure 3.6 shows the air masses that affect the climate of the British Isles. Describe the weather associated with each air mass.

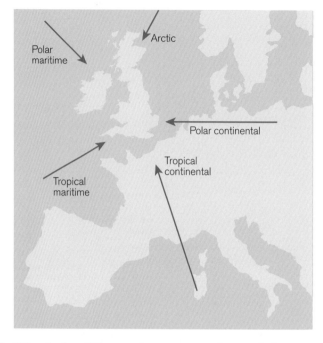

Figure 3.6 Air masses affecting the British Isles

8 What is the difference between weather and climate?

9 Define the following meteorological terms:
  a mid-latitude depression
  b anticyclone
  c front

10 Figure 3.7 shows the weather records for the Malham Tarn Field Centre taken in 1992. Malham Tarn is in the Yorkshire Dales.
  a Describe the climate experienced at Malham in 1992.
  b Are the statistics from Malham that are shown in Figure 3.7 typical of the cool temperate western maritime climate?

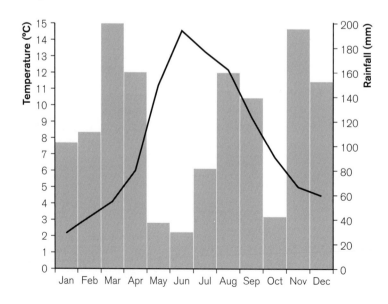

Figure 3.7 Weather record for Malham Tarn Field Centre (380m) in 1992

11 Describe the weather experienced when a depression passes over an area.

12 a Study the synoptic chart, Figure 3.8, and describe the differences in the weather experienced at weather stations A and B.

b How is the weather associated with a winter anticyclone different from that associated with an anticyclone in summer?

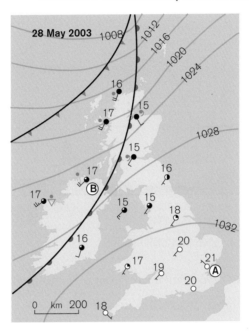

Figure 3.8 Synoptic chart for 28 May 2003

Weather symbols		Cloud cover		Wind speed	
• Rain	≡ Fog	○ No cloud	◑ 5 oktas	◎ Calm	∟ 8–12 knots
ʾ Drizzle	= Mist	◐ 1 okta	◕ 6 oktas	— 1–2 knots	∟ 13–17 knots
▽ Rain shower	✳ Snow	◔ 2 oktas	◕ 7 oktas	⊥ 3–7 knots	⊔ 18–22 knots
℞ Thunderstorm	△ Hail	◕ 3 oktas	● 8 oktas	For each additional half feather, add 5 knots	
		◑ 4 oktas	⊗ Sky obscured		

13 Describe the impact of any storm event in the cool temperate western margin climate that you have studied.

14 Describe the general features of one of the following climates:

a equatorial

b tropical wet and dry

c tropical monsoon

15 What is the inter-tropical convergence zone (ITCZ)? How does it move on an annual basis?

16 What conditions are required for tropical revolving storms (hurricanes/typhoons/cyclones) to develop?

Hint

17 Take the conditions from your answer to Question 16 and then ask where in the world you would find such conditions.

17 What is the worldwide distribution of the storms covered in Question 16?

18 Describe the impact that tropical revolving storms can have in areas they affect.

19 How can people manage the hazard of tropical revolving storms?

20 What is an 'urban heat island', and how does it come about?

21 Study Figure 3.9, which shows a typical urban heat island profile. Describe and explain the shape of the profile.

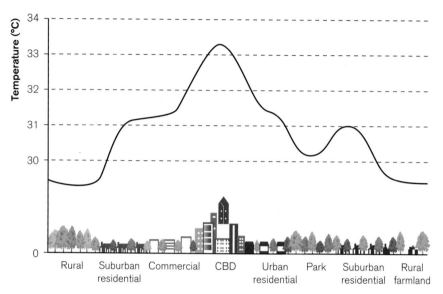

Figure 3.9 An urban heat island profile

22 How does precipitation vary from urban to rural areas?

23 How do urban areas affect winds?

24 What do you understand by (a) particulate pollution and (b) photochemical smog?

25 How have authorities tried to control atmospheric pollution in urban areas?

26 Describe some of the sources that are used to show evidence of climatic change and the reconstruction of past climates.

27 Describe some of the theories that have been put forward in an attempt to explain climatic change.

28 What could be the possible effects of current global warming on the British Isles?

29 What can be done at a local scale in order to slow, or even reverse, global warming?

30 Study Figure 3.10, which shows carbon footprints for selected countries in 2004.
   a What do you understand by the term 'carbon footprint'?
   b Suggest reasons for the differences shown.

Figure 3.10 Carbon footprints for selected countries, 2004

Topic **3.3**

Ecosystems: change and challenge

Things to learn

★ **Nature of ecosystems: structure of ecosystems, energy flows, trophic levels, food chains and food webs.** Make sure that you know the meaning of each of these terms and are able to support each term with knowledge of an example. Within the context of energy flows, you should study nutrient cycling and consider the use of Gersmehl diagrams.

★ **Ecosystems in the British Isles over time: succession and climatic climax illustrated by one of lithosere, psammosere, hydrosere or halosere.** You should be able to define both 'succession' and 'climatic climax'. For one of the plant successions identified you should know the characteristic features of the vegetation, including plant species, at each stage in the succession (see below).

★ **Characteristics of the climatic climax: temperate deciduous woodland biome.** You should know the key characteristics of the biome — composition and structure. You should also be aware of some of the local variations in the biome as this will add depth to your answers.

★ **The effects of human activity on succession, illustrated by one plagioclimax such as heather moorland.** You should know the meaning of the term 'plagioclimax' and the characteristic features, including plant species, of your chosen plagioclimax (see below).

★ **The biome of one tropical region (savanna grassland or tropical monsoon forest or tropical equatorial rainforest): the main characteristics of the biome.** You should know something about the climate and the soils of the biome, as well as the vegetation. You should be able to name species, and give a detailed description of the structure of the vegetation. You should know some regional or local variations within the biome as this will add depth to your answers.

★ **Ecological responses to the climate and soil moisture budget: adaptations by vegetation and animals.** You should know the meaning of the term 'soil moisture budget'.

★ **Ecosystem issues on a local scale: impact of human activity; urban niches.** You should know the meaning of 'urban niche', and be able to give an example.

> Note that the study of heather moorland is not compulsory — it is given as an example.

Things to understand

Ecosystems in the British Isles over time

Succession and climatic climax, illustrated by one of lithosere, psammosere, hydrosere or halosere. Make sure that you understand the processes behind the transition from one species to another in the chosen succession. You should also understand the links between the process and the species.

The effects of human activity on succession, illustrated by one plagioclimax such as heather moorland. You should understand the effects of human activity in modifying the plant species in the chosen plagioclimax (see below).

The biome of *one* tropical region (savanna grassland *or* tropical monsoon forest *or* tropical equatorial rainforest):

★ **Ecological responses to the climate and soil moisture budget — adaptations by vegetation and animals.** You should understand how plants adapt to the climate of the chosen biome. Make sure that you can refer to individual species and to the variations in adaptations between them.

★ **Human activity and its impact on the biome.** An understanding of the processes involved is the key element here. You should be able to refer to more than one type of human activity, making sure that the impact of each is distinct.

★ **Development issues in the biome, to include aspects of biodiversity and the potential for sustainability.** You should have a clear understanding of the terms 'development', 'biodiversity' and 'sustainability' and of how each term applies to the chosen biome. You should be able to give examples of where

> Note that the specification refers to both vegetation and animals.

> Note that there is an overlap here with the section on management of fragile environments. It would be a good idea to ensure that one of the case studies required in the latter comes from the chosen tropical biome, although this is not a requirement.

development is taking place and also to comment on its effects on biodiversity and sustainability.

Ecosystem issues on a local scale; impact of human activity:
★ **Changes in ecosystems resulting from urbanisation.** You should understand a range of ways in which the growth of urban areas and the increase of population in urban areas has impacted on ecosystems. Here, breadth is more important than depth.
★ **Colonisation of wasteland: the development of distinctive ecologies along routeways (e.g. roads and railways).** The planned and unplanned introduction of new species and the impact of this on ecosystems. The key elements here are processes. What processes operate on wasteland and routeways to make their ecologies different, and how are they distinctive? Where have new species been introduced in a planned context (e.g. parks and gardens) and in an unplanned context (e.g. escapees from parks and gardens)? What processes have caused both of these to occur?
★ **Changes in the rural–urban fringe.** Understand a range of ways in which vegetation has changed in the rural–urban fringe — for example, golf courses, landscaped science parks, designated development sites. Here, breadth is more important than depth.

Ecosystem issues on a global scale: the relationships between human activity, biodiversity and sustainability. You should understand each of these terms. The themes should be examined in general and at a global scale before moving on to the case studies.

Key case studies

★ You should undertake a case study about the effects of human activity on succession, illustrated by one plagioclimax such as heather moorland. You should study one local-scale case study area in the UK where your chosen plagioclimax is located — for example, parts of the North York Moors could be used for heather moorland or Salisbury Plain for chalk grasslands.

★ You should carry out one case study on an ecological conservation area. This case study should be at a local scale and concern the impact of human activity on the area. There are many examples in the UK and elsewhere in the world where 'green' areas are being protected from urban expansion or new 'green' areas are being created on former industrial sites. Note that such an area does not have to be within an urban area — the key aspect is that it is small in scale.

★ You have to study the management of fragile environments in terms of conservation versus exploitation. You should undertake *two* contrasting case studies of recent (within the last 30 years) management schemes in such environments. The key elements here are 'management', 'fragility' and 'contrasting'. It is recommended that each case study is on a regional to local scale, and that one is based in your chosen tropical biome. The other should come from any other area of the world. Examples include the Everglades of Florida, the Okovango swamps in Botswana, the Serengeti National Park, the Sundarbans in Bangladesh, the Comoros Islands, and there are many more. Each area chosen should be subject to pressures in terms of development (exploitation) with, at the same time, people wishing to protect it (conservation). Therefore, a balance needs to be struck between the two processes so that the various attitudes towards these can emerge. Questions asked will focus on the processes of management, conservation and exploitation, and the extent to which these processes can exist alongside each other.

Testing your knowledge and understanding

1 What is an ecosystem?

2 What is meant by the term 'trophic level'?

3 Describe how nutrients move within an ecosystem.

4 Study Figure 3.11. It shows a food web within an Australian tropical rainforest. Describe the main features of this food web.

Hint

3 One way to approach this is to draw a diagram to illustrate your answer. A Gersmehl diagram is one such technique.

The **answers** to the **questions** are on pages 110–114

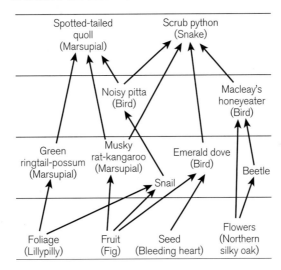

Figure 3.11 Food web

5 Define the terms 'succession' and 'climatic climax'.

6 Describe and explain one plant succession you have studied.

7 Describe the main characteristics of a temperate deciduous woodland.

8 Distinguish between the composition of a woodland and the structure of a woodland.

9 What is the meaning of the term 'plagioclimax'? Give an example of a plagioclimax in the British Isles.

10 Study Figure 3.12. Comment on the impact of human activity on species diversity on Salisbury Plain.

Hints

6 Note the two commands here — a good answer would provide clear linkages between the two elements of the question.

8 Make sure you make clear the differences between the two terms — provide connecting words, such as 'whereas, however…'.

Hint

10 Look at the diagram in detail — the relationship is not clear cut.

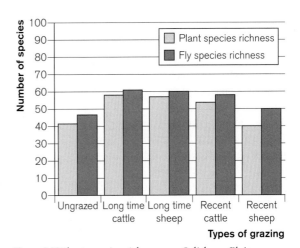

Figure 3.12 Plant species richness on Salisbury Plain

11 Describe the characteristics of one plagioclimax in the British Isles that you have studied.

12 Choose one tropical biome you have studied and describe the main characteristics of its vegetation.

13 With the aid of a diagram, explain what a soil moisture budget graph is.

14 Explain how plants in your chosen tropical biome have adapted to the climate.

15 Study the table below, which shows tropical rainforest data for selected countries. Comment on the loss of rainforest between 1990 and 2000 in the countries shown.

		Forest area (000 ha)	Forest as a % of total area	Forest change (000 ha) 1990–2000	% change 1990–2000
Africa	Cameroon	23 858	51.3	−222	0.94
	DR Congo	22 060	64.6	−17	0.08
Southeast Asia	Papua New Guinea	30 601	67.6	−113	0.36
	Malaysia	19 292	58.7	−237	1.20
South America	Brazil	543 905	64.3	−2309	0.42
	Guyana	16 879	78.5	−49	0.29

16 Define the term biodiversity, and comment on the level of biodiversity in your chosen tropical biome.

17 Assess the effect of development on the potential for sustainability within your chosen tropical biome.

18 In the context of ecosystems, define the term 'urban niche'.

19 Describe two changes that urban growth has brought to ecosystems.

20 In what ways is the colonisation of wasteland different from the development of a normal plant succession?

21 Outline how distinctive ecologies develop along a routeway of your choice.

22 Describe one planned way in which new species of plants have been introduced into an area.

23 Outline the impact of the unplanned introduction of species of plants into an area you have studied.

24 Describe changes in the vegetation of the rural–urban fringe that you have studied.

25 Evaluate the success of one ecological conservation area that you have studied.

26 Outline the main threats to biodiversity on a global scale.

27 In the context of vegetation, explain the meaning of the terms 'fragile', 'conservation' and 'exploitation'.

28 Study Figure 3.13, which shows the management plan for the Komodo National Park, Indonesia (the home of the Komodo dragon). Comment on the issues that could arise from the plan.

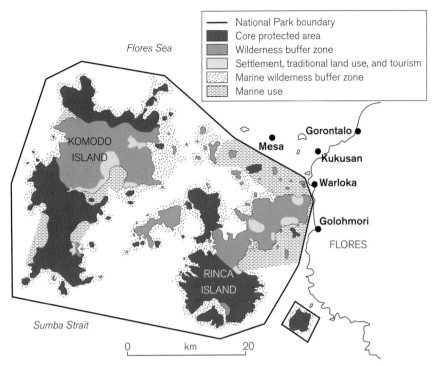

Figure 3.13 Komodo National Park, Indonesia

Hint

30 This is an open-ended question and the outcome will depend on your chosen environment. Make sure that you give some indication of 'extent to which'.

29 Compare the effectiveness of the two management strategies of fragile environments that you have studied.

30 Discuss the extent to which conservation and exploitation can co-exist in a fragile environment of your choice.

Topic **3.4**

World cities

Things to learn

★ **The global pattern: millionaire cities, mega cities and world cities**. You should know the meaning of each of these terms and be able to provide an example of each.

★ **Contemporary urbanisation processes: urbanisation; suburbanisation; counterurbanisation; re-urbanisation.** You should learn the meaning of each of these terms and be prepared to describe the differences between them. You also need to know details of a case study of each process (see page 59).

★ **Urban decline and regeneration within urban areas** (urban regeneration — gentrification, property-led regeneration schemes, partnership schemes between local and national governments and the private sector). You should learn the meaning of each of these terms and be prepared to describe the differences between them. You also need to know details of a case study of each process (see page 59).

Things to understand

Economic development and change related to urbanisation. This requires an overview of the relationship between the two concepts. To what extent are the two processes mutually dependent? You should be able to point to areas where more economic development has gone hand-in-hand with increased urbanisation. You should also be able to provide exemplars of where this relationship is not as direct.

Contemporary urbanisation processes:
★ Urbanisation — characteristics, causes and effects
★ Suburbanisation — characteristics, causes and effects
★ Counterurbanisation — characteristics, causes and effects
★ Re-urbanisation — characteristics, causes and effects

Each of these elements of the specification is discrete, and hence questions could be set on any one of them. There could also be questions that require comparison between two or more of the processes. You should be able to separate out each of the three elements required for each process: characteristics, causes and effects. For example, what are the characteristic features of a suburbanised area of a city, why has counterurbanisation taken place and what are the effects of re-urbanisation? Each process should also be studied in the context of a case study. Taken together, the case studies should cover a range of countries at different levels of development.

★ Planning and management issues — these two concepts should also be applied to each of the four urbanisation processes given above. How do planners and managers within cities respond to the processes and their effects? What do they put in place as a consequence of the occurrence of urbanisation processes? In addition, some of the processes are interrelated. For example, rapid urbanisation of an area may result in the growth of spontaneous settlements (shanty towns), which may in turn result in redevelopment of such areas with the purpose of re-urbanisation (encouraging the movement in of a certain type of person on to land previously occupied by shanty towns).

> This is an example of a management response that is planned. ▶

Urban decline and regeneration within urban areas:
★ **Characteristics and causes of urban decline.** You should be able to separate out the two elements of urban decline that are given here: characteristics and causes. It may be easier to focus on inner-city areas that have shown social, economic and environmental decline in recent years. Here, the characteristics of decline are easier to identify, as are the causes. A case study is not required, but references to actual areas always improve the quality of an examination answer.

> Each term is enshrined with a UK context, so the role of government at national and local level within the UK should be considered. ▶

★ **Urban regeneration** (gentrification, property-led regeneration schemes, partnership schemes between local and national governments and the private sector). The strategies and processes that make each of these distinctive should be studied in general and in the context of a case study of each (see opposite). A key element of each of these schemes is the degree to which they have been successful — questions will ask for some assessment or evaluation of their success.

Retailing and other services:
★ The decentralisation of retailing and other services — causes and impacts
★ The redevelopment of urban centres — impacts and responses

Both these processes relate to changes in retailing — one being an outward movement of shops and services and the other being a desire to retain shops and services within the CBDs of towns and cities. You should understand the factors that have given rise to both processes. The two processes should be examined in a general context, but references to actual areas would enhance the quality of any response (see case studies opposite). You should also be prepared for questions that ask you to evaluate the success (or otherwise) of each process within the context of a located area.

Contemporary sustainability issues in urban areas:
- ★ Waste management — recycling and its alternatives
- ★ Transport and its management — the development of integrated, efficient and sustainable systems

These two issues should be studied in general and with reference to a range of areas and locations where characteristic features of each issue are evident. The location of these exemplars can be anywhere in the world and it would be beneficial to use a selection that support a varied argument. For example, a case study of an effective form of waste management would be appropriate, as would a case study of a modern integrated transport system such as the Sheffield Supertram. Hence, depth of understanding is as important as breadth. You should also be prepared for questions that ask you to evaluate the success (or otherwise) of these schemes.

Key case studies

- ★ You should cover at least four different case studies of contemporary urbanisation processes — one for each of urbanisation, suburbanisation, counterurbanisation and re-urbanisation. The four case studies should cover a range of countries at different levels of economic development — for example:
  - urbanisation in Mumbai
  - suburbanisation in south Manchester
  - counterurbanisation in villages in Normandy
  - re-urbanisation in London Docklands

- ★ Although not a stated requirement of the specification it would be beneficial to study urban decline and each of the processes of urban regeneration (gentrification, property-led regeneration schemes, partnership schemes between local and national governments and the private sector) in the context of a named case study. It is likely that all such case studies will be based in the UK.

- ★ You should carry out one case study of an out-of-town retailing area and one case study of an urban centre that has undergone redevelopment. Details of the characteristics of each should be studied including the nature of the retail and service outlets, the types of transport systems to the areas, the design and layout of the buildings and the issues that have arisen there.

 ## Testing your knowledge and understanding

1 Describe the global distribution of millionaire cities.

2 Distinguish between mega cities and world cities, giving an example of each.

3 Describe and comment on the changing population sizes of the mega cities shown in the table below.

Hint

3 The command 'comment on' requires you to say something beyond description – what can you infer from the data that is geographical?

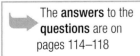 The **answers** to the **questions** are on pages 114–118

Ranking	Mega city	Population (millions)			
		1975	2000	2005	2015
1	Tokyo	26.6	34.4	35.2	35.5
2	Mexico City	10.7	18.1	19.4	21.6
3	New York	15.9	17.8	18.7	19.9
4	São Paulo	9.6	17.1	18.3	20.5

Hint

A starting point might be to classify the cities into groups — for example, developed, developing, European, North American.

Ranking	Mega city	Population (millions)			
		1975	2000	2005	2015
5	Mumbai	7.1	16.1	18.2	21.9
6	Delhi	4.4	12.4	15.0	18.6
7	Shanghai	7.3	13.2	14.5	17.2
8	Kolkata	7.9	13.1	14.3	17.0
9	Jakarta	4.8	11.1	13.2	16.8
10	Buenos Aires	8.7	11.8	12.6	13.4
11	Dhaka	2.2	10.2	12.4	16.8
12	Los Angeles	8.9	11.8	12.3	13.1
13	Karachi	4.0	10.0	11.6	15.2
14	Rio de Janeiro	7.6	10.8	11.5	12.8
15	Osaka	9.8	11.2	11.3	11.3
16	Cairo	6.4	10.4	11.1	13.1
17	Lagos	1.9	8.4	10.9	16.1
18	Beijing	6.0	9.8	10.7	12.9
19	Manila	5.0	10.0	10.7	12.9
20	Moscow	7.6	10.1	10.7	11.0

Hint

4 Beware of questions such as this — they are not always straightforward to answer. You are being asked to reflect on the relationship stated.

Hints

For each of Questions **6**, **7** and **8** you should refer to some specific detail that applies to a city you have studied.

Hint

9 The command word 'comment' requires you to consider the data and to then make a statement that is not directly evident, but is geographical.

4 'Rates of urbanisation increase as levels of development increase'. To what extent is this statement true?

5 Define each of the following terms: urbanisation, suburbanisation and counter-urbanisation.

6 For one named city that you have studied, explain why it has grown in size.

7 For one named city that you have studied, describe the effects of urbanisation on the character of the city.

8 How are the effects of urbanisation being managed in the city you studied?

9 Study the table below, which shows the districts of Bangalore in India. Describe and comment on the variations that exist among the different districts within Bangalore.

District	Chickpet	Basavanagudi	Bagular	Indiranagar	Yelankha
Description of area	Thriving commercial area; traffic congestion in narrow streets	Tree-lined avenues; well-off families living in detached houses and apartment blocks	Many migrants; public taps and washing areas; high crime rates	Large gated mansions; expensive shops in malls; well-qualified professionals, many of whom work for high-tech companies	An area of squatters; land at risk from flooding from river; no clean water or sanitation; unskilled and unemployed workers
Settlement age (years)	300	100	45	25	5
% of newcomers (moved in within the last 2 years)	2	10	65	20	80
Population density — persons per hectare	800	230	1200	150	1500

District	Chickpet	Basavanagudi	Bagular	Indiranagar	Yelankha
% literacy	78	80	45	99	10
Quality of life index (max 100)	55	70	35	98	15

Hints

11 Make sure that you focus on differences.
12 Refer to more than one type of technology.
14 Name a scheme, state what took place, and say whether it was a success or not.
15 The command word 'comment' requires you to consider the data and to then make a statement that is not directly evident, but is geographical.

10 Describe the impact of suburbanisation on an area you have studied.

11 In what ways is the impact of counterurbanisation on an area different from that of suburbanisation?

12 Discuss the role of technology in the process of counterurbanisation.

13 What is meant by the term 're-urbanisation'?

14 Evaluate the success of a regeneration scheme in a city you have studied.

15 Study Figure 3.14, which shows part of a redeveloped area in Cardiff's Old Brewery Quarter. Describe and comment on the redevelopment that has taken place.

Figure 3.14

Hint

17 It is always better to support general points with named examples.

16 Give four characteristics of an urban area that has declined.

17 Explain why some parts of cities have declined.

18 What is gentrification, and how can it be identified?

19 Distinguish between property-led regeneration and partnership schemes.

Hints

20 Consider more than one reason.
21 Make sure that you consider more than one type of impact. As well as negative impacts there are some that are positive.
22 You should consider a range of issues: social, economic, environmental.
24 Consider more than one response.

20 Why have many retailing areas been established out of town centres?

21 What has been the impact of the decentralisation of retailing on the central areas of towns?

22 What issues have the decentralisation of retailing had on the out-of-town area affected?

23 Describe the characteristics of one out-of-town retailing area you have studied.

24 In what ways have town centres responded to the development of out-of-town retailing areas?

25 Outline the main features of the redevelopment of one town centre you have studied.

26 Describe three ways in which urban areas manage their waste.

27 Study Figure 3.15, which shows the problem of refuse disposal in China. Comment on the issues raised.

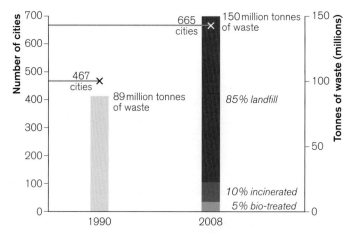

Figure 3.15 Refuse disposal, China

Hint

28 This question (and Question 30) is best answered with references to named areas of study. You can opt to choose either one city in detail (depth) or a number of cities in less detail (breadth).

28 To what extent can recycling be organised on a city-wide scale?

29 Outline problems associated with transport in urban areas.

30 Assess the effectiveness of one transport management system you have studied.

Topic 3.5 Development and globalisation

Things to learn

★ **The different ways in which development can be expressed** (economic, demographic, social, political and cultural)

★ **How to measure development.** You should know the meaning of GDP and GNP, how to calculate the human development index (HDI) and other ways of measuring development.

★ **Categories of development.** You should know the meaning of the terms 'first world', 'second world' and 'third world'. You should also know the terms 'developed' and 'developing' when applied to countries, and other terms such as least developed countries (LDC), newly industrialising(ed) countries (NIC),

Can you put a number of country names in each of these categories?

recently industrialised countries (RIC), centrally planned economies and oil-rich countries.

* **The meaning of the term 'globalisation' and the negative and positive impacts globalisation has on the world**
* **The progress of globalisation**
* **Global marketing**
* **Flows of capital, labour, products and services**
* **Patterns of production, distribution and consumption**
* **The growth of newly industrialised(ing) countries (NIC), particularly at the initial phase in the 'Asian Tiger' economies (Singapore, Hong Kong, South Korea and Taiwan)**
* **Further growth of NICs with India and China** (see overleaf under case studies)
* **Globalisation of services**
* **Growth of NICs in the twenty-first century with new markets and new technologies.** Reference should be made to at least one example — Brazil, Russia or Dubai should be considered (see below under case studies).
* **The poorest countries of the world and how they suffer in terms of quality of life, debt and various social problems.** You should know at least one good example.
* **The concept of the North–South divide**
* **The growth of the EU** (see overleaf under case studies)
* **Groupings of nations.** You should be able to refer to free trade areas, custom unions, common markets and economic unions.
* **The characteristics and spatial organisation of TNCs**
* **The growth of TNCs**
* **The social, economic and environmental impacts of TNCs in both host and donor countries**
* **The processes of trade and aid**
* **Definitions of economic and environmental sustainability**
* **The basic principles of ecotourism**

Things to understand

The development continuum. You should know the meaning of this term and understand how the continuum has come about.

Globalisation. You should understand the processes that have shaped globalisation and its development, such as free market ideas, deregulation of markets, GATT and WTO, trade blocs and the IMF and World Bank.

Global marketing. You should understand the development of global marketing and its relationship to patterns of production, distribution and consumption.

Initial NICs. You should understand how the initial NICs were able to develop and how companies set up by those countries eventually became TNCs.

Second wave of NICs. You should understand this development — for example, Malaysia.

The economic growth of China

The growth of India. You should understand how this economy grew, based largely on its service sector.

Growth in the twenty-first century. As growth is ongoing, it is important that you keep your material up to date. For example, if you take Dubai, you should be aware of its recent financial difficulties.

Countries at low levels of economic development (LDC). You should understand how such countries arrived in this situation and what steps are being taken, by themselves and by outside agencies, to improve the situation.

The North–South divide. You should understand the relationship between the North–South divide and the development continuum.

The consequences of the groupings of nations. You should understand the consequences in both positive and negative terms.

The impact of TNCs. You should understand the varied economic, social and environmental impacts in those countries in which TNCs choose to operate and in their countries of origin.

Trade and aid. You should understand the argument between trade and aid in terms of which can be of greater benefit to the economic development of poorer countries.

Economic and environmental sustainability. You should understand the question of whether economic sustainability can be compatible with environmental sustainability.

Sustainable tourism. You should understand the principle of sustainable tourism and whether it can ever be a widespread reality.

Key case studies

★ You have to undertake a case study of one TNC. This should cover its history, characteristics (what it does, products etc.), spatial organisation and its impact, both in its country of origin and where it operates. If this is essentially a manufacturing TNC, then it might be advisable to take a brief look at a service TNC (retailing, financial services) to see whether or not they operate in a different way.

★ Under **Patterns and processes** in the specification document it states that you should study the 'further growth of NICs, with particular reference to China'. The implication is that you must make a study of the economic growth of that country. If 'China' appears in the specification document, then examiners are entitled to make reference to it when setting questions.
  - The same applies to the next entry in the specification, which asks you to study 'globalisation of services, with particular reference to India'. Therefore, you need to make a study of the Indian service sector.
  - In the next section, the specification refers to 'Growth in the twenty-first century — the impact of new markets and new technologies (for example in Brazil, Russia and oil-producing countries)'. The best way to tackle this section is to look at the emerging economy and markets of one of those countries. A manageable case study is that of Dubai (be sure that you bring material on Dubai right up to date, such as knowing about its financial troubles in recent times).

★ In the section called **Global social and economic groupings**, the specification asks you to study 'reasons for the social and economic groupings of nations, with particular reference to the EU'. As the EU is named on the specification document, you are required to know certain facets of this organisation, in particular its growth and the reasons behind that growth.

Testing your knowledge and understanding

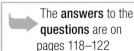

The **answers** to the **questions** are on pages 118–122

1 Define the following terms:
   a GDP
   b third world
   c NIC

2 What do you understand by the term 'development gap'?

3 What do you understand by the term 'development continuum'?

4 What is globalisation?

Hints

5 Which countries are known today for their manufacturing industry? Think of where it all began.

7 What attracted European and North American firms to want to invest in such countries?

5 How has the global distribution of manufacturing changed in the last 60 years?

6 What is 'global marketing'?

7 In the initial phase of the development of NICs, the 'Asian Tigers' (Hong Kong, South Korea, Singapore, Taiwan) were the first to emerge. What advantages did these countries possess for the development of manufacturing industry?

8 After the initial phase of NIC development what caused a second generation of NICs to emerge?

9 Figure 3.16 shows the amount of foreign direct investment into China between 1984 and 2003. Why were foreign companies keen to make such investments?

Hint

Think of a previous question. What are foreign firms looking for in China?

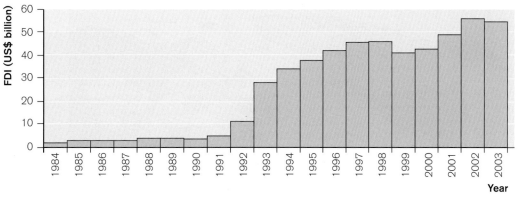

Figure 3.16 Foreign direct investment into China

10 How was India's growth as a NIC different from other countries?

11 What is happening to NIC development in the twenty-first century?

Hint

Remember that you are dealing with three separate groups of Indian people: rural people, urban people and the two groups combined to give a picture of the whole country.

12 What does Figure 3.17 tell you about poverty in India between 1973 and 2000?

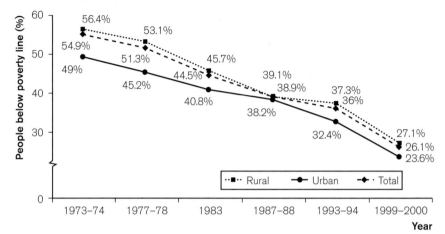

Figure 3.17 India: percentage of population below poverty line, 1973–2000 (people living on less than $1 per day)

13 By what criteria are countries judged to be least developed (LDC)?

14 Why is the quality of life so low in LDCs?

Hint

15 Think of the geographical position of such countries and then refer to their stability (politics, tensions etc.).

15 Not only do LDCs have economic and social problems, they also suffer from other problems. Describe some of these.

16 How can LDCs get out of their debt problems?

17 Why do countries form themselves into social and economic groups?

18 Describe the growth of the EU.

19 What can be the negative consequences of countries grouping together?

20 What is a transnational corporation (TNC)?

Hint

21 Costs are always going to be important, but in this case Nissan is seeking something more. It needs to manufacture in countries such as the UK and the USA. Why?

21 Nissan is a manufacturer of motor vehicles, with headquarters in Japan. Figure 3.18 shows the countries in which Nissan has manufacturing plants. Try to explain this distribution.

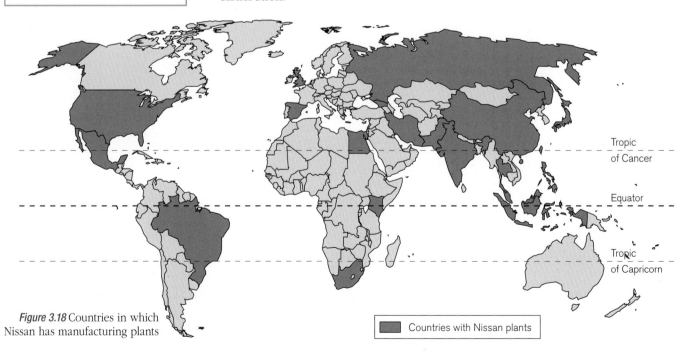

Figure 3.18 Countries in which Nissan has manufacturing plants

Countries with Nissan plants

22 Study Figure 3.19, which is part of a recent report (September 2009) on foreign direct investment (FDI) in India. What type of FDI does India attract and why is the country such an important destination for investment?

> Improving global sentiment and a growing conducive environment in India are increasingly facilitating foreign investors' role in the country. Several other factors being attributable to the revival of FDI in the country include liberal investment policies and reforms, innovative and technologically advanced products being manufactured in India and low cost and effective solutions.
>
> India has been ranked in third place in global FDI this year, following the economic meltdown, and will continue to remain among the top five attractive destinations for international investors during the next two years according to a report by UNCTAD. In July 2009, FDI inflow into India was $3.5 billion, 56% higher than in the same month the year before according to the Commerce and Industry Ministry. The services sector comprising financial and non-financial services attracted nearly $1.9 billion in the April–June period along with over $200 million in the computer software and hardware sector. The Indian retail market, which is the fifth largest retail destination globally, has been ranked the most attractive emerging market for investment by the retail sector according to a recent report by the Global Retailing Development Index.

Figure 3.19 FDI report

23 How important globally is the service sector in foreign direct investment?

24 When TNCs locate their plants overseas, what impacts can this have on the countries in which they locate?

25 When a TNC locates overseas, how can this decision have an impact on the country in which it was first established?

26 What are the main systems through which aid can be supplied?

27 In what ways can aid be distributed to those in need of it?

28 Efforts to create development in developing countries have often centred around two different approaches, namely trade and aid. State the main arguments put forward for both and indicate how some critics feel that they do not work in this context.

29 What is the difference between economic and environmental sustainability?

30 What is sustainable tourism?

Hints

26 Focus on the type of supplier.
30 Refer to a general explanation of the term 'sustainability', and then apply that definition to tourism.

Topic **3.6**

Contemporary conflicts and challenges

Things to learn

Bear in mind that some of the words can apply to the same area and conflict.

★ **The nature and origin of conflict: identity (nationalism, regionalism, localism), ethnicity, culture, resources including territory, ideology.** You should know the meaning of each of these words, be able to put them into a geographical context and know an example for each that applies in a conflict situation.

★ **Patterns of conflict: national, regional and local.** Make sure that you know the meaning of these terms and have knowledge of areas where they apply.

★ **Expression of conflict: non-violent, political activity, debate, terrorism, insurrection, war.** Make sure that you know the meaning of these terms with knowledge of areas where they apply.

★ **The geographical distribution of cultural groupings in the UK.** You should be clear as to the cultural groupings whose distribution you are describing. It may be easier to learn about the distributions of various ethnic groups within the UK.

★ **The global distribution of poverty.** You should know the meaning of the term 'poverty' and the various ways in which it can be recognised.

> The UK census remains a good starting point, although there are updated sources of information on the internet through GIS-based data sources.

Things to understand

Conflict resolution. Conflict resolution has to be an active, planned process that is a major role of governments at all levels. Governments must (proactively) plan to reduce the potential for conflict. Governments must also have frameworks and institutions to (reactively) manage conflict. You should understand more than one process of conflict resolution.

The challenge of multicultural societies in the UK: reasons for the development of multicultural societies and issues related to multicultural societies. Many of the questions on this topic will ask you to 'discuss', 'analyse', 'evaluate'. Make sure that you are able to write about several reasons and issues, and can demonstrate some evidence of critical understanding. It is always better to reinforce the points you make with references to actual places.

> Note that this topic has to be studied in the context of the UK.

Separatism within and/or across national boundaries: its nature, reasons for its occurrence and its consequences. You should understand the characteristics of separatist pressures in a range of locations around the world, and the reasons for their development. By covering a range of such pressures and locations you should be able to discuss the similarities and differences between them. You should also study a range of separatist pressures the consequences of which vary from violent to non-violent.

> It would be a good idea to make a detailed study of one area where separatist pressures exist.

The causes of poverty. You should understand that poverty exists at a variety of scales around the world and that it can be measured in several ways. You should understand the mechanisms by which areas become poor and be able to discuss the interrelationships between them.

> It is always better to support your discussion with references to places around the world.

Addressing poverty on a global scale, including the work by international agencies such as the United Nations. Note the context for this is global, so only global strategies should be considered. You could examine the work of NGOs such as charitable organisations, the work of supranational groupings such as the G8 and G20, and the United Nations (required in the specification). The UN Millennium Development Goals (MDGs) should be studied. Evaluation material for these is regularly updated on the internet.

Key case studies

★ You should study a conflict over the use of a local resource (e.g. land, buildings, space). The conflict could be in your area, where you undertake fieldwork, or where, if not local, the details of the conflict are easily available. Examples could include the building of an airport runway or terminal, a new shopping complex, a new housing area, a bypass around a village, a wind farm, a golf course and there are many others. You should make sure you can answer questions on each of the following three elements:

– the reason for the conflict and the attitudes of different groups of people to it
– the processes that operate to resolve the conflict
– recognise that, when the outcome is decided, some people benefit whereas others may lose

Hence, it is a good idea if the conflict has been either 'running' for a few years or has ended.

★ You have to undertake one or more case studies involving the social, economic and environmental issues associated with major international conflicts that have taken place within the last 30 years. In particular, you should study one major international conflict that has taken place (or is taking place) and consider the effects that the conflict has had (or is having) on the geography of the area affected. An international conflict is one that involves more than one country, either as combatants or as peacemakers. Examples include conflicts in the Gaza Strip, the West Bank, Israel, Iraq, Afghanistan, the Darfur region of Sudan, East Timor, the contested region of Kashmir in India/Pakistan. Make sure that you understand the difference between the terms 'social', 'economic' and 'environmental' when considering the impacts as questions could be set on each of these elements as well as the interrelationships between them.

★ One detailed case study about **Separatism within and/or across national boundaries** should be undertaken. Make sure that you cover the nature of the separatist pressures, reasons why they developed and their consequences for the region in which they occur.

★ The issue: **'No development without security, and no security without development'** should be discussed in the context of an actual area. The only aspect of choice is the nature of that area. You could choose to study this in the context of an area such as Bangladesh where farmers lack security of tenure and security against the force of nature, and hence further development of their lands is difficult. 'Security' could be interpreted in a more military sense. Areas such as Afghanistan and Zimbabwe have difficulty ensuring security against internal combatants, which makes increased development more challenging for the local populations. Be prepared to discuss the alternative viewpoints that have arisen and are stated openly in the quotation.

Testing your knowledge and understanding

Hints

1 Make sure you are clear in your understanding of the terms 'nationalism' and 'regionalism'.
2 Make sure you are clear in your understanding of the terms 'ethnicity', 'territory' and 'ideology'.

The **answers** to the **questions** are on pages 122–126

1 Give the meaning of the following by referring to an example of each:
   a conflict caused by nationalism
   b conflict caused by regionalism

2 Give the meaning of the following by referring to an example of each:
   a conflict caused by differences in ethnicity
   b conflict over resources, including territory
   c conflict over ideology

3 Distinguish between the terms 'international', 'national', 'regional' and 'local'.

4 Describe the differences between terrorism and insurrection.

Hints

5 Remember to exemplify each of these with the name of an area where it is occurring/has occurred.

7 The main ways in which this is done is by planning processes. However, these are not straight-forward — be aware of their complexity.

8 You should consider world-orientated organisations.

9 Make sure that you refer to the participants by specific titles or names, and not by generic labels such as environmentalists, planners, or even worse, 'some people'.

12 For each of Questions 10, 11 and 12 you must be sure of the meanings of the key words — environmental impacts, standard of living, economy.

5 Research these additional terms in conflict geography: 'invasion' and 'ethnic cleansing'.

6 Give an example of an area where conflict is manifested by political debate.

7 Explain how conflict can be resolved at a local level.

8 Outline the nature of global systems of conflict resolution.

9 You will have studied one conflict over the use of a local resource. Answer the following questions about that conflict.
   a Describe the background to the conflict.
   b Describe and suggest reasons for the varying views of participants in the conflict.
   c Evaluate the outcome, or potential outcome, of the conflict.

10 For one major international conflict you have studied, describe the environmental impacts of the conflict on the area affected.

11 For one major international conflict you have studied, discuss how the standard of living of the participants in the conflict has been influenced.

12 For one major international conflict you have studied, assess the extent to which the economy of the area has been affected.

13 What is a multicultural society?

14 Give reasons for the development of multicultural societies in the UK.

15 Study Figure 3.20. Describe the geographical distribution of the Asian population within York.

Figure 3.20 Distribution of the Asian population in York, 2001 (1 dot = 1 person)

16 Describe how, and suggest why, the geographical distribution of one cultural grouping within the UK has changed over time.

17 By referring to one or more example, outline the consequences of two issues associated with multicultural societies in the area(s) you identify.

18 Identify and describe one benefit associated with multicultural society in the UK.

19 What is meant by the terms 'separatism' and 'autonomy'?

20 Give three examples in the world where separatist pressures exist.

21 Outline three distinct reasons for the development of separatist pressures.

22 Write about one area of the world where separatist pressures have been violent and one where they have been non-violent.

23 How can poverty be measured?

24 Study Figure 3.21. To what extent does it illustrate the distribution of poverty in the world?

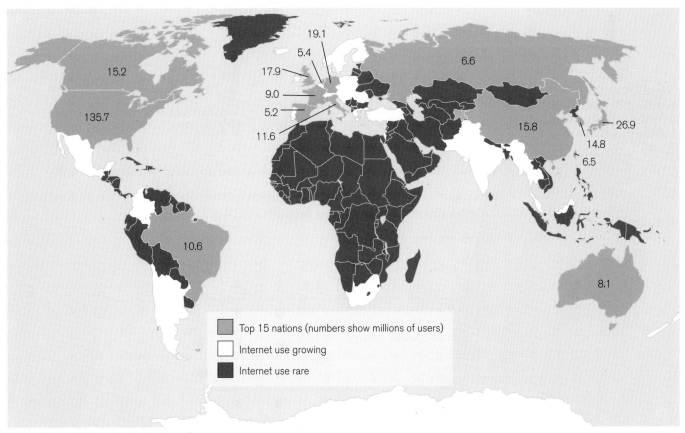

Figure 3.21 Global distribution of internet users, 2007

25 Explain the causes of poverty in the world and comment on the interrelationships between them.

Hint

26 The command 'comment on' requires you to consider the data, and then make a statement that is not directly evident, but is geographical.

26 Study Figure 3.22. Describe and comment on the changes to poverty levels in different areas of the world between 1990 and 2005.

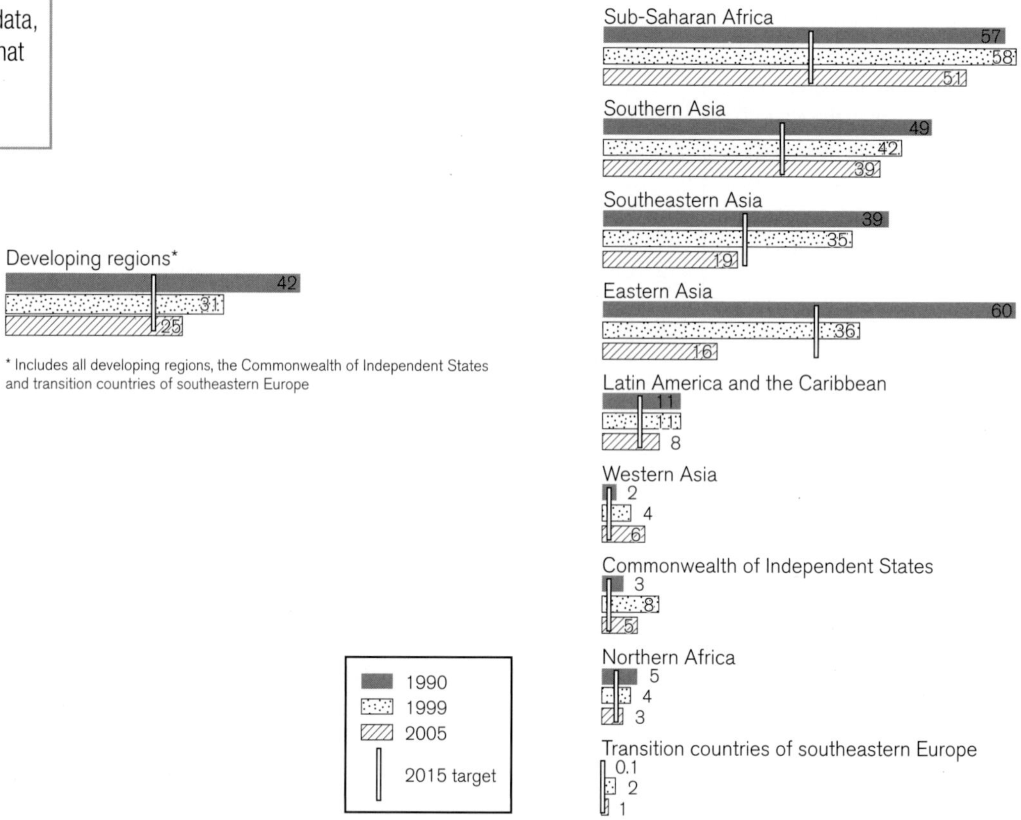

Sub-Saharan Africa
57
58
51

Southern Asia
49
42
39

Southeastern Asia
39
35
19

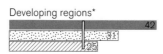

Developing regions*
42
31
25

* Includes all developing regions, the Commonwealth of Independent States and transition countries of southeastern Europe

Eastern Asia
60
36
16

Latin America and the Caribbean
11
11
8

Western Asia
2
4
6

Commonwealth of Independent States
3
8
5

	1990
	1999
	2005
	2015 target

Northern Africa
5
4
3

Figure 3.22 World poverty levels, 1990–2005 (percentage proportion of people living on less than $1.25 a day)

Transition countries of southeastern Europe
0.1
2
1

27 What is the G8 group of nations? Assess its role in addressing global poverty.

28 Suggest reasons for the variable progress towards reaching the Millennium Development Goals shown in Figure 3.23.

MDG	India	Brazil	Egypt	Bangladesh
1 Eradicate extreme poverty and hunger	○	●	◐	○
2 Achieve universal primary education	○	●	◐	◐
3 Promote gender equality and empower women	○	●	○	●
4 Reduce child mortality	⊖	◐	◐	○
5 Improve maternal health	○	◐	◐	○
6 Combat HIV/AIDS, malaria and other diseases	⊖	●	◐	○

● MDG reached by 2007

◐ MDG likely to be reached by 2015

○ MDG not likely to be reached by 2015

⊖ Not enough data

Figure 3.23 Progress towards selected Millennium Development Goals in four countries

Hints

For Questions **29** and **30**, you need to decide on the scale of the area that will form the context of your answer. It could be national, or regional, or even local.

29 Write an account of one area in the world where development is being held back by a lack of security.

30 Write an account of one area in the world where development is being encouraged in order to achieve greater stability in the area.

Answers

Unit 1 Physical and human geography

Rivers, floods and management

1 A drainage basin is the area from which a river system obtains its water. It is also referred to as its catchment area. Drainage basins are bounded by imaginary lines called watersheds, which separate one drainage basin from another.

2 The main input is precipitation, along with energy from the sun for evaporation. Outputs are evaporation from surfaces and transpiration from plants (collectively called evapotranspiration), runoff into a larger drainage basin or into the sea, and percolation deep into underground stores where it can be lost from the system.

3 Interception is where precipitation is prevented from directly reaching the surface by plants, particularly the leaves and branches of trees. Some of this water is evaporated off the surface of the plants, becoming an output, and does not continue through the drainage basin system.

4 Base flow is that part of a river's discharge that is produced by groundwater seeping slowly into the river. It is the element that maintains the river when it does not rain for a long period.

5 The area should be shaded as water surplus. This is because 80 mm has been removed from the soil between May and September. After 80 mm of precipitation has fallen in excess of evapotranspiration from September onwards, the water balance is back in surplus.

6 River discharge is the volume of water passing a measuring point in a river in a given time. To measure discharge you need to find the cross-sectional area of the river at the measuring point and the speed of the river at that point. Take the cross-section in square metres and the speed in metres per second and multiply them to give a figure in cubic metres per second (cumecs), which is the discharge.

7 Discharge is affected by the following:
   - the intensity and duration of the precipitation event
   - antecedent precipitation
   - type of precipitation — snow, for example, can be stored on the ground and only find its way as runoff when it melts

   - soil and rock type — porous or impermeable
   - size and shape of the drainage basin
   - slope angles within the basin
   - temperature — high temperatures will increase the rate of evapotranspiration
   - type of vegetation cover (or lack of it)
   - land use
   - level of urbanisation in catchment area

8 a Approximately 5 hours
   b Approximately 36/37 cumecs
   c These factors indicate that there was very little interception of the rainfall by vegetation, and that water did not soak into the ground but ran quickly down the slopes into the river.
   d Figure 1.3 indicates that there was heavy rainfall at the start of this period. There were two segments of 15 minutes when over 10 mm of rain fell in each and one segment of nearly 10 mm. In total, around 70 mm of rain fell in just over 4 hours. This also accounts for the very steep rising limb, indicating serious flooding in the area.

9 Rivers erode through the following processes:

   hydraulic action — the sheer power of moving water

   abrasion — scraping, scouring and rubbing of the river's load along its sides and bed

   attrition — the reduction in size of the load as a result of abrasion

   corrosion — the process at work on rocks that contain carbonates, e.g. limestone; minerals are dissolved by the weak acid in river water

10 **Capacity** is the amount of material a river can carry as load at any given time.

   Competence is the diameter of the largest particle that can be carried for a given velocity.

11 The transport of load is carried out by the following processes:
   - **traction** — large debris rolled and pushed down the bed of the river
   - **saltation** — smaller stones are bounced down the channel
   - **suspension** — very small particles are carried in the water and moved along by the force of the flow, which gives many rivers a brown appearance

- **solution** — minerals are dissolved and then transported in the mass of water

12 Rivers begin to deposit their load when they lose energy and are no longer competent to transport it. This can occur when there is a reduction in gradient; where the river's discharge is reduced; when the water enters a shallow part of the river (e.g. inside of a meander); when there is an increase in the size of particles (possibly due to a tributary river bringing in larger particles); when the river floods (it overtops its banks and flows with decreased velocity across a floodplain).

13 a At the start of the section the sediment is dominated by angular rather than rounded sediments. Angular pieces there account for 75% of all sediments. As one passes down the section the rounded material increases until at the end, rounded pieces form 70% of all sediment, a complete reversal from the situation at the beginning of the section. Between 7 km and 9 km though, the angular pieces are in the majority for a short distance.

b It is possible that the main river is joined here by a tributary carrying a higher level of angular fragments than the main river. These fragments are gradually eroded by attrition as they pass down the main river, so the rounded fragments are again in the majority downstream of this point.

14 Variations in the long profile can be explained in terms of:
- **gradient** — steep in the upper valley, gentle in the lower part
- **varying rock types** — resistant rocks produce kinks in the long profile
- **lakes and reservoirs** — flatten out the profile
- **rejuvenation** — steepens part of the long profile

15 Channel shape is described by the **hydraulic radius**. This is calculated as:

$$\text{hydraulic radius} = \frac{\text{cross-sectional area of the channel}}{\text{wetted perimeter}}$$

A high hydraulic radius means that the river is efficient. This is because the moving water loses proportionately less energy in overcoming friction.

16 Stream A has a hydraulic radius of 2.22.
Stream B has a hydraulic radius of 1.66.
Channel A is more efficient.

17 A rough and uneven channel that is lined with boulders creates friction. This slows down the velocity of a river. Rough channels are found in the upper course as channel roughness decreases with increased distance downstream.

18 Braiding occurs when the river is forced to split into several channels. It is most likely to occur when a river has a variable discharge. A sudden fall in discharge causes the river to deposit its load in the channel. This is a typical feature of rivers in semi-arid areas and of glacial streams with variable annual discharge.

19 The floodplain is the result of both erosion and deposition. The width of the plain is produced by meander migration causing lateral erosion. This creates a bluff line at either side when the interlocking spurs have been removed. Each time the river floods across this plain, layers of alluvium are deposited.

20 Deltas form when a river enters the sea or a lake. As the velocity of the river decreases so does its sediment-carrying capacity, therefore the load is dropped. On entering the sea, flocculation occurs as fresh water mixes with seawater. Clay particles then coagulate and settle on the bed. Not all rivers produce a delta in such circumstances. For it to happen, the sediment load of the river has to be high and the coastal area into which the river is flowing has to have a low tidal range and weak currents. Therefore, rivers flowing into lakes often produce deltas.

21 Rejuvenation is when a river renews its capacity to erode as its potential energy increases. This occurs when there is either a fall in sea level relative to the level of the land or a rise of land relative to the sea. The river then adjusts to its new base level by cutting into its existing valley.

22 In a river valley with well-developed meanders, rejuvenation causes increased vertical erosion resulting in the meanders being deepened or incised. When incision is slow, some lateral erosion also takes place resulting in **ingrown meanders**. With rapid incision, downcutting dominates and a steep-sided, gorge-like valley is formed (**entrenched meander**).

23 The physical causes of flooding are:
- large amounts of precipitation over a prolonged period of time leading to the saturation of the soil

- intensive precipitation over a very short period of time, particularly when the ground is baked hard from a long period of drought
- the rapid melting of snow
- large amounts of precipitation from certain weather events such as hurricanes and deep mid-latitude low-pressure systems

24 The main impacts of human activities on flooding are:

urbanisation — concrete and tarmac create impermeable surfaces allowing faster runoff; less vegetation in urban areas means less interception; surface water is channelled directly into drains; bridges can restrict river flow also allowing debris to build up underneath them

building on the floodplain

deforestation — less interception and water taken up through the roots; greater risk of soil erosion allowing more sediment into rivers, which obstructs the flow

25 Hydrologists try to forecast the likelihood of future flood events using past records. They use river-discharge records in relation to precipitation and flood-recurrence-interval graphs. Flood recurrence interval is plotted against discharge on scattergraphs (on semi-logarithmic paper), and using the line of best fit it is possible to predict how often floods of a certain magnitude are likely to occur.

26 The most obvious contrast is between the impact in a developed country such as the UK and a developing country such as Bangladesh. Your assessment of the impact should be divided under headings:
- transport
- agriculture/industry
- housing
- power and water supplies
- disease
- loss of life
- impact on different levels in society
- overall cost

27 Hard engineering often involves extensive modification to the river's channel or to the floodplain. Such solutions include:
- dams
- embankments (levées)
- channelisation of the existing channel (e.g. straightening, concreting)
- dredging for channel enlargement
- flood-relief channels
- flood-storage reservoirs

28 Soft engineering for flood management includes ways of slowing down the rate at which water enters the channel, and reducing the amount of water. Such schemes are sustainable — the basin is managed in ways that consider the whole area, they avoid damaging the environment as they work with it and they are not the eyesore that many hard-engineering schemes present. Such schemes include afforestation, agricultural land-use management, land-use zoning, wetland and riverbank conservation and river restoration schemes.

29 The impact was as follows:
- 7000 residential properties were flooded
- 1300 businesses were flooded
- one person died
- £250 million of insurance damage
- 2000 families had a considerable loss as they had no contents insurance
- 3500 council houses and 12 schools were severely damaged and had no insurance to cover that damage

30 It has been predicted that global warming could increase rainfall leading to river flooding. This is because higher temperatures will result in increased evaporation over the seas and oceans leading to greater precipitation. It could also increase the severity of tropical storm systems and the rainfall associated with them. Polar ice cap melting will lead to rising sea levels which would inundate low-lying floodplains and deltas.

Cold environments

1 Today, ice sheets cover Antarctica and Greenland. Small ice sheets, known as ice caps, are found in areas of Iceland, Norway and Spitsbergen.

2 The lower edge of the area of permanent snow in upland areas. As a climate becomes colder, the snow line moves down the slope.

3 The snow line on European mountains is lower in altitude in summer on north-facing slopes. This is because the south-facing slopes receive more insolation because they face the sun. This means that at the same height, the temperatures are higher on the south-facing side than on the north-facing side.

4 Snow, falling initially as flakes with an open feathery structure, accumulates on mountains, and compression by the upper layers gradually turns the lower snow into a more compact mass known as neve or firn. Meltwater seeps into the gaps and then freezes, further compacting the mass.

5 Types of flow include:
- compressing flow, which occurs when there is a reduction in the valley floor gradient — ice decelerates and thickens
- extending flow, which occurs when the valley floor becomes steeper — ice accelerates and becomes thinner with crevasses forming
- rotational flow within the corrie, with the ice pivoting about a central point in the hollow
- basal flow, which involves friction at the base of the ice bringing about some melting; the resulting meltwater acts as a lubricant enabling more rapid flow

6 As the ice moves forward the upper ice tends to move faster than the ice below. This is the zone where crevasses form as sections of ice move faster than the ice behind. At the base of the glacier there is friction between the ice and bedrock which slows the ice. The lower layers also may be frozen into the bedrock which again slows its progress.

7 A glacier can be viewed as a system in that it has inputs, stores, transfers and outputs. The inputs are precipitation in the form of ice and snow and avalanches which add snow, ice and debris from the valley side; storage is the glacier itself; transfer is ice movement; the outputs are water vapour, calving, debris deposited at the snout and ablation (melting).

8 a Ablation is the wasting of the glacier mainly by melting. Sublimation also occurs on the surface, which changes the ice directly into water vapour.
  b As autumn temperatures decrease, ablation gradually decreases. With colder temperatures there is more snow therefore more accumulation. This gradually increases the mass of the glacier. With winter accumulation and little ablation, glacier mass is highest at the end of winter through into spring. With increasing temperatures and declining snowfall, glacial mass declines through the summer and is lowest in autumn.

9 Glacial mass shrinks. As the mass is not as extensive, this is reflected by the end of the glacier (snout)

being found closer to the source. The glacier appears to retreat up its valley.

10 **Abrasion** occurs when the material the glacier is carrying rubs away at the valley floor and sides. **Plucking** involves the glacier freezing onto and into rocks. As the ice moves forward, it pulls masses of rocks away at the base and sides of a valley. Some of this material is then used during the abrasion process.

11 The main features are: armchair-shaped hollow; steep backwall; over-deepened basin; rock lip; possible moraine on lip; rocky backwall with scree at base; occupied by small lake (tarn). To reach the higher levels of a mark scheme, examiners need to see some quantification. The tolerance limits normally accepted by examiners for corries are: diameter, 0.5–1 km; backwall/depth, 100–400 m; backwall angle, between 60° and vertical.

12 A pyramidal peak. The sides represent corries where rotational sliding of the ice has produced steep hollows on the sides of mountains. In this case, the erosion has been so intense that instead of a hollow only the steep backwall remains divided from the adjoining corries by the knife-edged ridges (arêtes) seen on the photograph. With two or more corries cutting back into the mountain, only the top pyramidal shape remains.

13 Glacial troughs have the following features:
- steep sides and flat bottoms — the typical U-shape
- usually fairly straight with a stepped long profile with alternating steps and rock basins
- some glacial valleys end abruptly at their heads in a steep wall known as a trough end
- rock basins may be filled with ribbon lakes at the side; hanging valleys are formed which often contain waterfalls plunging to the main valley floor
- the spurs from the existing river valley will have been removed to form truncated spurs
- small areas of rock on the valley floor which the glacier failed to remove are known as roches mountonnées
- immediately after formation, many glacial troughs are occupied by shallow lakes forming behind rock barriers; in time, these are filled by deposits to form a flat valley floor
- quantification on width: examiners usually accept anything from 0.5–3 km

14 **Roches moutonnées** are formed by glacial erosion and are therefore formed of solid rock. They

represent sections of the valley floor that the glacier did not remove. They have a gentle slope on the upstream side and a steep slope on the downstream side. **Drumlins** are depositional features formed underneath the ice that consist of boulder clay (unsorted till). They have a steep upstream side and a shallower side on the downstream side.

15 Glaciers transport debris in one of three positions:
- on the surface of the ice — **supraglacial**
- buried within the ice — **englacial**
- at the base of the ice or between the ice and the bedrock — **subglacial**

Another way to describe it is to call material at the side of the glacier lateral moraine, material in the centre of the glacier medial moraine and material at the base, ground moraine.

16 a A terminal moraine marks the furthest extent of a glacier or ice sheet. At this point, large amounts of debris are deposited forming a ridge-like feature running parallel to the ice front.
   b As a glacier retreats, it is possible for a series of morainic ridges to be formed, each marking a point where the retreat halted for some time. These are recessional moraines.

17 The main difference is that fluvioglacial material is sorted (by water) and is distinct from unsorted glacial deposits. Fluvioglacial material can also be laid down in layers as opposed to glacial material which is usually dumped as a mass.

18 a From east to west
   b An esker
   c After forming the recessional moraine, the glacial snout retreated towards the east. Meltwater from the glacier could not flow west as it was blocked by the moraine (if it occupied the whole width of the valley). The meltwater collected behind the moraine and formed a lake, on whose floor deposits accumulated. As the water level reached the top of the moraine it overflowed cutting a stream valley, which slowly lowered the outlet until the lake was completely drained. The lake deposits are the evidence of its previous existence.

19 Outwash plains are the material deposited beyond the snout of a glacier by the meltwater streams that issue from it. Outwash consists of a gently sloping plain made up of sands and gravels. These particles are graded into different sizes, the larger ones

being found near to the ice front, and becoming progressively finer with increasing distance from it. The finest particles, rock flour, may be transported considerable distances before being deposited.

20 The permafrost is that part of the ground that is permanently frozen. This can reach great depths, at least 1500 m in parts of Siberia. The upper layers in the tundra are not part of the permafrost as they thaw in summer (active layer). Permafrost can be continuous, discontinuous or sporadic, depending mainly on the temperature of an area.

21 a In frost shattering (freeze–thaw action), water in cracks freezes at night and since ice occupies more space than water (about 10% more) pressure is exerted on the crack which widens. Repetition over a long period cracks rock surfaces.
   b In nivation, freeze–thaw and chemical weathering operating under the snow cause the surface to disintegrate. Snow melt and solifluction carries particles downslope eventually creating a small hollow on the hillside.

22 When the active layer above the permafrost thaws in summer, excessive lubrication reduces the friction between soil particles. Even on very shallow slopes, particles begin the move downslope. This forms large sheets or lobes of land on valley sides in tundra areas, sometimes forming terraces on valley sides. It was a widespread process in southern England during the Quaternary glaciation.

23 A climate and vegetation type found in the most northerly parts of Eurasia and North America. Tundra-type environments occur above the tree line in mountainous areas such as the Alps, Rockies, Andes and Himalayas. They are also found in extreme southerly areas such as Antarctica and islands such as South Georgia. The climate is characterised by long, very cold winters; brief mild summers; 8 months when the temperature is below zero; small amounts of precipitation. The vegetation has an extremely low net primary productivity; very few plant species, therefore low biological diversity; absence of fully grown trees; many plants are ground hugging; slow growth rates; perennials.

24 The tundra is considered to be fragile because of its limited productivity. The slow rate of plant growth means that any disruption to the ecosystem takes a long time to be corrected. Low productivity combined with limited species diversity means that plants are

very specialised and any disruption causes difficulty when it comes to regeneration. Disruption to the functioning of the biome, therefore, has long-term implications.

25 The traditional economic activity of the population was hunting and fishing, particularly in North America where the Inuits hunted and fished for seals, whales and occasionally hunted polar bears. In Europe, the Lapps followed the seasonal movements of herds of wild reindeer and lived off them, with fishing supplementing their diet. The environment provided all that the people of the tundra needed. The low population density put little pressure on the environment and their lifestyle was, therefore, completely sustainable.

26 In recent years, the tundra has been exploited through mining (particularly for oil), hydroelectric power (HEP), fishing and tourism. In the northern hemisphere, the strategic position of Alaska, northern Canada and Siberia has given rise to a considerable amount of military activity.

27 The low temperatures, short summers, low precipitation, thin and stony soils, permafrost, the active layer (waterlogging) and blizzards have all impacted upon human habitation and the exploitation of the region. Some of the solutions have been:
- to elevate buildings on piles (driven into the permafrost) above the soil allowing air circulation and heat removal into the atmosphere and not the ground
- to build larger structures on aggregate pads, which also reduces transfer of heat into the ground
- insulated boxes (utilidors) to hold pipes carrying water supplies, heat and sewage

28 After the collapse of fur sealing at the beginning of the nineteenth century, the focus of attention switched to whales. With a reduction of the whale population in the North Atlantic, whalers turned their attention to the Southern Ocean looking mainly for blue and right whales. This became a highly profitable business with major stations on South Georgia and the South Shetlands. Whale stocks became seriously depleted and the industry collapsed in the twentieth century. Fishing has replaced whaling, although concerns have been expressed regarding over exploitation. Tourism is a modern economic activity with over 40 000 people visiting the area every year, mainly on cruise ships.

29 Damage that could be caused by large numbers of tourists includes the following:
- The ecosystem is extremely fragile, so disturbances would leave an imprint for a long time.
- The peak tourist season coincides with peak wildlife breeding periods, so wildlife could be affected adversely.
- Pressure on the few ice-free locations on the continent.
- Over-flying by light planes and helicopters can cause stress to breeding colonies.

30 There are a number of treaties and protocols designed to control the economic development of the area. In an attempt to control fishing in the area and preserve fish stocks for the future, limits on catches are set by the Convention on the Conservation of Antarctic Marine Living Resources (CCAMLR). With tourism, there is the International Association of Antarctic Tour Operators (IAATO), whose aim is to minimise tourist impact because much of the scientific value of Antarctica will be lost if it is polluted or significantly disturbed. The British Antarctic Survey (BAS) see themselves as being in the role of stewardship, working to the highest environmental standards in all their operations. The Protocol on Environmental Protection in the Antarctic Treaty of 1991 sets out tight rules governing human activities on the continent. Development is, therefore, sustainable if the conditions set out in the various treaties and agreements are kept.

Coastal environments

1 This is an upland coastline that faces north and east. The main physical features are:
- Runswick Bay
- headlands, such as Kettleness
- cliffs
- beaches
- wave-cut platforms

Descriptions should be organised by types of feature (e.g. erosional, depositional) rather than by their geographical location on the coast. It is important to refer to specific map evidence, such as place names and/or feature names.

2 Note that you should concentrate on one landform in the area. Headlands and bays can be explained in terms of the variable resistance of rocks to marine erosion and the distribution of wave energy along the coasts (i.e. high energy on headlands, low energy

in bays). Cliffs can be explained by the relief of the coast, erosion and the resistance of rocks to erosion and sub-aerial processes. Cliff recession is responsible for the formation of wave-cut platforms. The beach in Runswick Bay appears to be swash-aligned and is associated with low-energy conditions and wave refraction.

3 These are sections of coastline where overall there is a balance between erosion and deposition. They are often split into sub-cells where there are specific inputs of materials whose transportation is then monitored. Clear boundaries define them, such as headlands. In theory, they represent closed systems. Thus, there is no transfer of material between the cells. There is a debate about the extent to which this is true. You should refer to an example to illustrate the concept.

4 Constructive waves are low waves with a long wavelength (low frequency), whereas destructive waves are high waves with a shorter wavelength (high frequency). Constructive waves have a gentle spill onto a beach whereas destructive are more plunging. For constructive waves, the swash has greater energy than the backwash; the opposite is the case for destructive waves. Destructive waves create a steeper beach profile.

5 Wave refraction. You should practise the diagram that illustrates this process because it is likely that you could be asked to draw it.

6 Waves erode in a number of ways:
- hydraulic action (wave quarrying) — the weakening effect of air trapped in a cliff face being forced to compress and then expand as waves hit repeatedly
- pounding — the sheer force of water itself (without debris) upon a rock surface, causing it to weaken
- abrasion/corrasion — the effect of the material the sea has picked up being hurled against a cliff line and intertidal rock platforms
- attrition — the rocks in the sea which carry out abrasion are slowly worn down into smaller and more rounded pieces

7 When waves approach the shore at an angle, material is pushed up the beach by the swash in the same direction as the wave approach. As the water runs back down the beach, the backwash drags material down the steepest gradient, which is generally at right angles to the beach line. Over a period of time,

sediment moves in this zig-zag fashion down the coast.

8 Sub-aerial weathering is where the effects of the weather on the land have an impact on the coast in such a way that rock is weakened by the process and subsequent removal is easier. Examples of processes include: solution, freeze–thaw, biological weathering and the action of salt crystals. Here, the evaporation of water in the rocks produces salt crystals that expand when they form and put stress upon rocks. Salt from sea water spray is capable of corroding several types of rock.

9 Spits are long, narrow ridges of sand and/or shingle that are attached to the land at one end — the proximal end. The distal end is in the sea and often extends partly across an estuary. This end can be hook-shaped and is likely to change position over time. Salt marsh often develops behind and sand dunes may be present. Exemplification of a spit would help here, with details of size. They form due to the presence of a lot of available material; the process of longshore drift, the dominance of constructive waves and the appropriate coastal configuration, i.e. the presence of an estuary or a change in direction of the coast.

10 Storm beach — at the back, near the cliff line — represents a ridge where material is thrown by swash during extreme conditions and thus, is above the level of high spring tides. Berms are formed by the swash during high tide. These ridges at the back of the beach represent the section highest up the beach where material was deposited in a particular tidal cycle. Cusps form where sand and shingle meet and the gradient begins to steepen. This is due to strong swash and stronger backwash. The strong scouring action removes material, especially from the centre of the semicircular depression, creating the cusp. Runnels are depressions in the sand between ridges that are left as the tide goes out. Their position is linked to the breakpoint of the waves.

11 Case study material is required here and the content will vary depending upon that selected. Examiners may expect to see references to Holderness, North Norfolk or areas of the south coast of the UK. Physical consequences involve the undercutting of cliffs leading to collapse; mass movement processes of slumping, sliding and falls are also significant. Loss of land is an end result, causing coastal retreat. Socioeconomic consequences that relate to the

knock-on effects of loss of land may also feature. In this context, these are only significant where there are either people present or major installations — farmland is not considered significant. Socioeconomic consequences include the loss of buildings, and even significant parts of settlements; issues of insurance; deaths/injuries; impact of the threat of loss and actual loss of home/livelihood.

12 Isostatic sea-level change concerns a localised change to sea level. During the major glaciations, the weight of the ice depressed the Earth's crust immediately beneath the ice. This caused a local relative rise in sea level. A eustatic sea-level change is one that is worldwide. The melting of ice sheets at the end of the ice ages caused a global rise in sea level as large quantities of water returned to the sea.

13 Rias are created by rising sea levels drowning river valleys. The floodplain of a river vanishes beneath the rising waters, but on the edges of uplands only the middle- and upper-course valleys are filled with sea water, leaving the higher land dry and producing this feature. In Devon and Cornwall, for example, sea level rose and drowned the valleys of the rivers flowing off Dartmoor and the uplands of Cornwall. Good examples are the Fowey estuary in Cornwall and the Kingsbridge estuary in south Devon. Rias have a long section and a cross profile typical of a river valley, and usually a dendritic system of drainage.

You could also write about fjords.

14 Raised beaches are areas of former wave-cut platforms and their beaches which are at a level higher than the present sea level. Behind the beach it is not unusual to find old cliff lines (called a relict cliff) with wave-cut notches, sea caves, arches and stacks. Raised beaches are common around the coasts of western Scotland, where three levels have been recognised, at 8 m, 15 m and 30 m. They have been caused by the land rising at a faster rate than the rise in sea level. Because of differential uplift in the region, these levels are only approximate.

15 A case study is required so responses will be determined by the particular study. Events could include: the 1953 floods in eastern England, or the Towyn floods, or floods elsewhere in the world. Impacts will be physical and human:
- physical — flooding of land, impact on farmland, salt water contamination, breaching of barriers

- human — deaths and injuries, homes lost, people evacuated, insurance claims

16 Coastal flooding can be prevented/managed by:
- the use of barriers across tidal rivers — for example, the Thames Barrier
- the use of warning systems and shelters — for example, in the coastal areas of Bangladesh
- the use of integrated management schemes involving dams, shipping channels, sluice gates, and natural defences, as in the Netherlands

17 Hard engineering involves the construction of man-made features to protect a coastline. This could involve sea walls, gabions, revetments, groynes and barrages. Soft engineering uses natural systems for coastal defence, such as beaches, dunes and salt marshes which can absorb and adjust to wave and tide energy. It involves manipulating and maintaining these systems, without changing their fundamental structures. Beach nourishment and dune regeneration are examples.

18 The coastal protection structures shown are gabions, sea walls and groynes. Gabions stabilise coastal slopes, reducing the threat of mass movements. Groynes promote the accumulation of beach sediments. Sea walls protect the coast from wave erosion. It is important to be clear what each structure is protecting and how. The gabions are protecting the slope by replacing it with a series of shallow terraces. The groynes are protecting the beach by allowing it to stay in place, thereby protecting the shoreline from erosion. The sea wall is protecting the shoreline from erosion by reflecting waves.

19 Rock armour (rip-rap) consists of large boulders dumped in front of a cliff or sea wall to take the full force of the waves.

Revetments are concrete or wooden structures placed across the beach to take the full force of wave energy.

20 Beach nourishment is an attempt to replace material that has been lost through longshore drift. It is not unknown for local councils to move material from one end of a beach to the other before the start of the tourist season.

21 The content will depend on the case study used. Material could relate to:
- beach nourishment (as above)

- dune regeneration — stabilising by erecting fences or using wire mesh, replanting marram grass and afforestation of conifers, restricted access, education for tourists
- managed retreat — involves abandoning the current line of sea defences and then developing the exposed land in some way, perhaps with salt marshes, to reduce wave power

22 Sand dunes: there are five areas of sand dunes that form narrow strips of deposits parallel to the coast. The widest is just north of Barmouth, the narrowest is near Tywyn. The longest continuous stretches are near Harlech and Barmouth, and the shortest is just south of Harlech. They are all on spits or south of an estuary. The salt marshes are found parallel to the rivers. The largest appears to be along the River Mawddach, extending over 20 km inland and nearly 5 km wide.

23 Coastal dunes are formed by the wind on the landward side of a beach. They form best where there is a wide foreshore that dries out between the tides. Strong onshore winds dry out the beach and remove large quantities of sand with which they build dunes. At first, embryo dunes develop which become colonised and stabilised by lyme grass initially and marram grass later. These then join up to create larger foredunes which frequently lie parallel to the shoreline. With time, other grasses, fescues and heath plants colonise the dunes producing a psammosere. Exposed areas of sand may become eroded by the wind to create blow-outs (dry) or slacks (moist).

24 A salt marsh is an area of vegetated tidal mudflats located within an estuary or on the landward side of a spit. Fine sediment accumulates in the sheltered water, which is then colonised by a sequence of salt-tolerant plants such as glasswort and *Spartina* as the level of the marsh is raised by further deposition. *Spartina* has two root systems — a fine mat of surface roots to bind the mud, and long, thick, deep roots that can secure it in up to 2 m of deposited material. The plants gradually develop a close vegetation over the mud and this allows colonisation by other plants such as sea aster, marsh grass and sea lavender. These form a dense mat of vegetation up to 15 cm high. The growth of vegetation has the effect of slowing the tidal currents even further. As the land rises above sea level, rushes and reeds become established.

25 When high and steep waves break at the foot of a cliff their erosive capabilities are concentrated into only a small area of the rock face. This concentration leads eventually to the cliff being undercut, forming a feature known as a wave-cut notch. Continued activity at this point increases the stress on the cliff and in time it collapses.

26 A wave-cut platform:
- is a gentle rock slope, often less than 5°
- appears smooth from a distance, but is deeply dissected on closer examination
- is rarely longer than 0.5 km from cliff to sea

27 Tens of millions of pounds are spent annually in the UK on coastal protection. It might be cheaper to let nature take its course and pay compensation to those affected. Large tracts of land could be 'surrendered to the sea' if trying to protect them is considered to be a waste of money.

28 Geological factors are important. When different rock types are arranged at right angles to the coast then the less resistant rocks are eroded faster to form bays and the more resistant rocks form headlands. This may be partly rectified by wave refraction with more powerful waves being concentrated on the headland, but in many areas this has less of an effect.

29 Tides are the periodic rise and fall in the level of the water in the oceans and seas. They are the result of the gravitational attraction of the sun and moon. The moon has the greatest influence, pulling water towards it to create a high tide, with a compensatory bulge on the opposite side of the Earth. In the intervening areas, the tide is at its lowest. Tides follow the 28-day lunar cycle. Every 28 days the gravitational pull is greatest and this gives the highest tides, known as spring tides. At the point in the cycle 14 days after this event, tides are at their lowest and then begin to rise again. This lowest point in the cycle is known as the neap tide.

30 Some alternative views could be:
- People who choose to live on coastlines where erosion and flooding risks are high must accept personal responsibility.
- If the principle of personal responsibility is abandoned, it could open the way for a large number of claims related to other natural hazards.
- If coastal management policies have changed, putting a community at risk from erosion and flooding, there could be a case for compensation.

- Where coastal engineering works have disrupted the sediment system and increased the risks of erosion or flooding, there could be a case for compensation.
- People living on the coast, unable to get insurance and through no fault of their own, could lose everything as a result of natural erosion or flooding.
- Few coastal communities are under immediate threat from erosion, therefore the number of people seeking compensation would always be small.

Hot desert environments and their margins

1 Arid describes a dry area, where the precipitation is less than 250 mm per year.

2 Evapotranspiration is the sum of **evaporation** (movement of water to the air from sources such as the soil, water bodies and canopy interception) and **transpiration** (the loss of water from plants through their stomata).

3 They are located within and just outside the tropics. In the southern hemisphere they are also found on the western sides of the continents of South America, Africa and Australia. Hot deserts are also found on the western side of North America.

4 The difference in temperature between the hottest point of the day and the coldest part of the night. With few clouds to block incoming solar radiation, insolation levels are high in desert areas during the day. At night, the lack of cloud cover allows long-wave radiation to escape, so temperatures fall rapidly.

5 Plants have adapted in a variety of ways, including measures to reduce moisture loss; storing water for long periods; searching for water over a wide area or at depth; having a short life cycle. The following features enable them to survive:
- fleshy stems/swollen leaves
- thick, waxy cuticles
- thick protective bark
- small, spiky leaves
- bulbous or very long roots
- salt tolerance

6 **Ephemerals** have a very short life cycle. They therefore avoid drought by only appearing when it rains. **Xerophytes** are adapted to withstand drought. They live permanently in the desert and adopt a number of strategies to prevent water loss and to store water over long periods.

7 Deserts are found where poleward moving air at high levels sinks towards the surface at around 20–30° north and south of the equator. This creates high pressure cells known as tropical anticyclones. Air moving towards the equator from the mid-latitudes also sinks there, reinforcing the high pressure. This creates clear, cloudless conditions. Deserts form on the western side of continents as the trade winds bring rainfall to the eastern sides.

8 Other factors include:
- continentality — places in inland regions usually have much lower rainfall than those in coastal areas
- relief — some very dry areas lie in the rain shadow of mountain areas
- cold ocean currents — air moving onshore crosses the current and is cooled. As the dew point is reached, condensation takes place at the lower level, producing fog. The fog is burnt off onshore by strong tropical insolation meaning that it is unlikely to rain in such coastal areas

9 As evapotranspiration exceeds precipitation, moisture is drawn upwards by capillary action. Salts and mineral bases (magnesium, sodium, calcium) are also drawn upwards and deposited in the upper layers to give a slightly alkaline soil. Crusts can also form on the surface.

10 There are four major forms in desert areas:
- **exfoliation** — heated exterior of rocks expands faster than cooler inside; the resulting stress cracks rocks parallel to the surface
- **granular disintegration** — different minerals expand and contract at different rates, stressing the rocks which then crack
- **shattering** — constant expansion and contraction on homogeneous rocks leads to shattering
- **block separation** — well-jointed rocks with prominent bedding planes break down into blocks when subject to constant expansion and contraction in the desert heat

11 Chemical weathering usually involves the presence of salts brought to the surface by capillary action. Weathering can involve:
- **crystal growth** — when water evaporates this causes expansion and results in surfaces cracking
- **hydration** — certain salts absorb water, leading to their expansion

- **solution** — soluble minerals dissolve when water is applied

12 The two types of erosion are:
- **deflation** — wind removes loose material from the surface
- **abrasion** — material carried in the wind sandblasts exposed rock surfaces

13 When the wind picks up loose surface material by the process of deflation, the finer material (sand etc.) is removed leaving behind the larger particles (small stones etc.). This rock-covered surface is known as the reg or desert pavement.

14 Labels that could be included are:
- **hard resistant layers** (on the layers protruding)
- **softer layers** (on indentations on pedestal)
- **abrasion greatest nearest ground** (on the lowest indentation)
- **wind strongest near ground** (on the lowest indentation, perhaps accompanied by an arrow to show turbulence and undercutting)

15 There are several ways in which the wind transports material:
- **suspension** — the finest material is carried along in the air and can be removed vast distances. Particles are normally less than 0.15 mm in diameter. A lot of material results in a sand storm.
- **saltation** — the wind moves particles forward in a bouncing motion. Grains are picked up, carried forward and dropped back to the surface and then the process is repeated
- **surface creep** — heavier material is rolled and pushed along the surface

16 When wind speed drops, it eventually falls to a point at which particles can no longer be carried. Material is then deposited, usually around some obstruction, as velocity is slowed on the downward side. Sand dunes are built up in this way. As the sand is rolled up one side of the gathering mound, it avalanches down the other side producing an asymmetric-shaped feature (gentle on the upwind side, steep on the downwind side). The dune therefore migrates in the direction of the prevailing wind. As the wind moves faster at the side of the mound (less sand to move), it carries the sand further producing two elongated features known as horns. This gives the barchan its classic crescent shape.

17 An exogenous river is one that rises outside of a hot desert area and then flows across it to emerge on the other side. Such rivers therefore flow all year (perennial). The Nile and Colorado Rivers are good examples.

18 A wadi is a channel in a desert area that has been formed by running water. They are steep-sided with broad flat bottoms and do not contain permanent streams or rivers. Lengths vary from a few metres to many kilometres. Channels on their floors are often braided, indicating the deposits of sediments and the changing course of flow after each flash flood, with which wadis are particularly associated.

19 Flooding occurs in desert areas as a result of rapid surface runoff, which could be caused by:
- very heavy rainfall in a short period of time
- rain exceeding the infiltration capacity of the ground
- the surface may be hard and baked
- little vegetation to provide interception of the runoff

This means that a large percentage of the rain that falls finds its way as runoff into river valleys (wadis).

20 This is a typical mesa-and-butte landscape. In areas of horizontal sedimentary rock, water and wind erosion eat gradually into the landscape, leaving behind sections of the original area. If the strata are horizontal, then the previous surface is likely to have been flat, plateau-like. Mesas are the remains of that flat-topped plateau; buttes are the remnants of the mesas when erosion and weathering are prolonged. On the lower slopes, scree, resulting from the mechanical weathering of the upper slopes can be seen, and also rockfall.

21 In desert areas, when streams (perennial or ephemeral) run down from an elevated area, material builds up where the stream meets the gentler slopes of the lowland. The rapid energy loss on the break in slope causes the load to be deposited. This deposition spreads out as an alluvial fan, with the stream dividing into distributaries to flow over it. When several streams run off an area, the alluvial fans created may coalesce to form a much larger unit known as a bahada.

22 Badlands are areas where soft and relatively impermeable rocks are moulded by rapid runoff. The main features of such landscapes are:
- many wadis with steep sides and flat bottoms covered by debris
- hillside gullies
- slope failure combined with slumping

- alluvial fans at the foot of slopes often forming bahadas
- pipes and caves formed when water passes underground
- natural arches formed by cave erosion

23 Desertification was defined by a United Nations conference in 1978 as 'the diminution or destruction of the biological potential of the land which can lead ultimately to desert-like conditions'. It can be brought about by both physical and man-made processes.

24 Climate change can bring about desertification in the following ways:
- less rainfall, both in total amounts and reliability
- less rainfall will lead to increased drought, both in frequency and intensity
- higher temperatures produce increased evaporation which reduces condensation and could lead to decreasing rainfall
- rivers and water holes dry up
- vegetation dies, robbing the land of its protective vegetation cover, thus exposing the soil to both wind and rain

25 Increasing population increases the pressure on the land for increased food production. Agricultural changes may lead to overcultivation, overgrazing and a removal of vegetation that cannot be re-established. All of this may expose the ground surface to wind and rain and consequent soil erosion, land degradation and, ultimately, desertification. In some areas the increasing demand for fuelwood for cooking (and heating) has stripped the land of its protective vegetation cover.

26 The Sahel is the name given to an area immediately south of the Sahara desert in Africa which runs from the Atlantic Ocean to the Horn of Africa. It covers parts of the following countries: Senegal, Mauritania, Burkina Faso, Mali, Niger, Chad, Sudan and Eritrea.

27 Some of the suggested causes have been:
- variation in rainfall over a long period of time with two periods of drought, one in the 1960s and the other in the 1970s
- population growth putting pressure on the land
- civil wars in Ethiopia and Eritrea
- settling of nomadic populations leading to overcultivation
- the widespread use of fuelwood for cooking (in many areas of the Sahel burning wood provides over 80% of energy needs)

28 Some of the initiatives have been:
- environmental rehabilitation schemes, e.g. agroforestry
- soil and water conservation, e.g. contour stone line building
- use of higher yielding drought-resistant crops
- small-scale irrigation schemes
- improved livestock programmes, including selected destocking programmes (Oxfam)
- early warning schemes to prevent the onset of drought-induced food shortages

29 a From 1947 to 1960, visitor numbers were small and hardly rose (in fact, they fell from 1954 to 1958). Subsequently, they rose fairly steadily through to the early 1980s, although there were several years when numbers were less than in the previous year. From the early 1980s, numbers began to rise dramatically from around 250 000 per year until the peaks in the mid-1990s where they reached over 850 000. There has been a slight decline since then, although numbers were rising again at the end of the period. Overall, numbers have increased substantially since 1947.

b The attractions of semi-arid areas for tourism could include:
- generally hot and dry conditions
- clear, cloudless skies, therefore plenty of sunshine
- variety of landscapes for sight-seeing, particularly features such as canyons, mesas, buttes, badlands, salt lakes and natural arches
- the weather and the low population density means that there is a high potential for outdoor activities
- plenty of space free from people, buildings and agriculture to construct hiking and biking trails

30 The answer is very similar to the answer to Question 29. The main reasons are the dry climate, all-year round sunshine (320 days per year at Phoenix (in Arizona)) and the potential for outdoor activities. In the USA, where water sources can be found, golf courses have been constructed in such environments.

Population change

1 **Birth rate** is a measure of a country's fertility. It is expressed in the number of live births per 1000 people in 1 year. **Fertility rate** is also a measure of fertility — it is the average number of children each woman in a population will bear. In such calculations, it is usual to refer to women between the ages of 15 and 45 (or 50). If fertility is 2.1 children,

then it is likely that a population will replace itself. Note that birth rate refers to a whole population, whereas fertility rate refers to part of a population.

2 **Infant mortality** is the number of deaths of children under the age of 1 year expressed per thousand live births per year. In the past, infant mortality claimed a considerable percentage of children born, but the rates have declined significantly in developed countries in modern times, due mainly to improvements in basic healthcare (e.g. sanitation), though technological medical advances (e.g. immunisation) have also helped. Some suggest that infant mortality indicates attitudes to child welfare — hence rates can also reflect the social development of a country.

3 a Order of development: D, B, A, C

b The indicators support country D as the most developed: low growth rate, low infant mortality rate (IMR), more elderly people and high life expectancy. Country C appears to be least developed: high IMR, 2% growth rate, low life expectancy. The evidence for B and A is more conflicting: growth rates are similar as are fertility rates, but B has lower IMR and longer life expectancy.

4 Population density might increase when there has been a natural increase in the area (caused by births being greater than deaths), or migration into the area. Conversely, density could decrease due to natural losses (e.g. a hazard or war) or emigration.

5 In many parts of the world, tradition demands high rates of reproduction. Intense cultural expectations may override the wishes of women, and they are expected to produce several children from an early age. In many Asian and sub-Saharan African countries, it is common for teenage girls to have had a child. On the other hand, education for women, particularly female literacy, is a driver towards lower fertility. With education comes knowledge of birth control, more opportunities for employment and wider choices. Family planning is becoming more widespread in developing countries and helps women avoid unintended pregnancies and lowers birth rates.

6 Death rates are lower in countries with higher levels of economic development. Poverty, poor nutrition, a lack of clean water and sanitation (all associated with low levels of economic development) increase mortality rates. Some infectious diseases have a

high impact on death rates in some parts of the world. For example, AIDS/HIV is having a significant effect on mortality in sub-Saharan Africa. In 2002, infectious diseases were responsible for 32% of global deaths, with AIDS, TB and malaria accounting for 10%; non-communicable diseases (NCD) (e.g. heart disease, strokes, cancers) were responsible for 59% of all global deaths. The risk of death from NCD is increasing globally. In 2005, NCD killed more people than AIDS, TB and malaria combined.

7 Thailand appears to have been at Stage 2 in 1960 as there was a significant gap between birth and deaths that continued until 1980. The birth rate is falling all the time, and the death rate begins to level out from 1970. At this point Thailand reaches Stage 3. Growth rates are stabilising at a low level, though the rate of decrease of birth rate is slowing down. Thailand cannot be said to be within Stage 4, as birth rates are still too high.

8 The population structure of a country in Stage 4 has a narrow base, whereas a country in Stage 2 has a broad base. In Stage 4, the pyramid has straight sides, and tapers only in the upper-age groups; in Stage 2, there is a steep tapering.

9 To some people, the DTM is useful because:
  ● it is universal in concept — it can be applied to all countries in the world, thereby making comparisons easier
  ● the timescales are flexible; indeed some suggest that level of development should be the key dependent variable

Two criticisms are:
  ● It is eurocentric. It is firmly based in the context of what happened to countries within the Western world.
  ● It ignores two important factors, namely the impact of government intervention in population control and the importance of cultural values and norms, especially with regard to the status of women.

10 Overall, the pyramid is projected to become straighter and less tapered by 2050. There are fewer people below the age of 50. This has been caused by a reduction in the birth rate over time. On the other hand, the proportion of elderly people has increased, with a significant increase in the ages 55 to 80. This is due to a fall in the death rate, as life expectancy increases. Significantly larger numbers of people in

their 90s will exist, especially females. The overall population of Poland is projected to decrease.

11 Forced migration occurs when a migrant has to move from a source area due to factors beyond his/her control. These may be natural, such as migrants leaving Montserrat during a volcanic eruption, or human, such as fleeing from a war zone, or from an area of unrest as when Kosovan people left Serbia. Voluntary migration occurs when the migrant makes the decision to move. Examples include Polish people moving to the UK to work, and elderly UK citizens moving to coastal Spain to retire.

12 Dependency ratios illustrate the degree to which the non-economically active population is dependent on the working population. In most countries shown the dependency ratios have either decreased or remained stable. This could be due to the size of the reduction in the number of children outnumbering the increased numbers of elderly.

Germany is an anomaly in that the ratio is increasing. This is probably due to an increasing elderly population. Issues that could have arisen include:
 • increasing cost to government of state pensions
 • increasing cost to government of healthcare for ageing populations

Declining birth rates cause problems of managing school closures.

13 Some countries such as those in the Middle East have youthful populations. In the short term, this may cause challenges in terms of education facilities — both teachers and buildings. Later, there are problems in providing enough jobs for the growing numbers of young adults. The consequences are that the young, and often the skilled, educated people, leave the country to work in more developed countries. Poland is another country that has a youthful population and has experienced out-migration. This then has the impact of reducing the numbers of carers for older people as they live longer.

14 Impacts of out-migration include:
 • The younger adult age groups (20–34) migrate, leaving behind an older population.
 • Males are more likely to migrate, causing an indentation on that side of the population pyramid.
 • Birth rates will fall and death rates will rise.

15 Inner London has a high percentage of young adults (20–39 years) who may have moved into the area for work. They are likely to be migrants from overseas, or from other parts of the UK. Eastbourne has more elderly people than the national average (25%). They are likely to be people who have moved to the town to retire.

16 In general, economic costs could include
 • the costs of educating the migrants' children have to be borne
 • that some industries are over-dependent on migrant labour
 • that much of the money earned is repatriated to the country of origin
 • that increased numbers of people add to the pressure on health services and education

Economic benefits could include
 • economic migrants tend to take up the less desirable jobs
 • the host country gains skilled labour at a reduced cost
 • the 'skills gap' that exists in many host countries is filled by qualified migrants
 • costs of retirement are transferred back to the country of origin

In answering such questions make sure that you refer to real places.

17 Overpopulation exists when there are too many people in an area relative to the amount of resources and the level of technology available locally to maintain a high standard of living. It implies that, with no change in the level of technology or natural resources, a reduction in the population would result in a rise in living standards. Underpopulation occurs when there are too few people in an area to use the resources efficiently for a given level of technology. In these circumstances, an increase in population would mean a more effective use of resources and increased living standards for all of the people.

18 For example: Julian Simon was an American economist who asserted that increasing world population was compatible with rising living standards, a view that was in direct contrast to the pessimism of Thomas Malthus and neo-Malthusianism. Simon argued that population increase benefits the world by enlarging the productive workforce and boosting productivity. He thought that shortages of vital resources pose no threat to mankind, and that, far from being a sign of impending disaster, scarcities often led to the development of better resources. Mankind's response to population growth had been, he held, the driving

force of civilisation through history. He predicted that while the world would become more populated, it would be more economically stable and less vulnerable to the disruption of resources. As a result, people would be richer and their lives less precarious.

19 Some large and highly populated countries have experienced a reduction in the percentage of undernourished people. In east and southeast Asia, there is a large block of countries that have experienced such a reduction. There is also a reduction in Brazil and in western South America, and in areas to the west in Africa. All of temperate South America has either a reduction or a continuously low percentage — a favourable situation.

There is an increase in the percentage of undernourished in a large, almost continuous, belt running through north, central, east and southern Africa. The situation appears to have deteriorated in a number of areas that have experienced 'setbacks'; if the percentage of undernourished has increased it is likely that there are more people who are now undernourished compared with 1990, although many of these are areas with relatively low population totals: western and central Africa, Bolivia, Paraguay.

Mexico (with a population of 110 million) and parts of Central America, Pakistan (population 160 million) and central Asian states such as Kazakhstan and Uzbekistan have all suffered an increase in the percentage of undernourished. There are general improvements in South America and eastern Asia; but the situation has deteriorated in much of Africa and western Asia. Large parts of the temperate 'north' and 'south' have a continuously low percentage of undernourished population.

However, it is difficult to assess overall progress on the basis of these data. Even those countries that have made progress could still have large numbers of undernourished — it all depends on the situation at the baseline in 1990 and the numbers involved.

20 For example in Thailand:
- The government set up the Population Development Agency (PDA).
- This was led by an economist and public relations expert (Mechai Viravaidya).
- There is widespread encouragement to use condoms, plus the use of the intravenous contraceptive DPMA.
- Free contraceptive services were extended to remote areas.

- The policy was supported by leaders of the Buddhist faith.
- Opportunities for sterilisation (vasectomies) are made available with incentives (e.g. free on the King's birthday).
- The PDA offered loans (for farmers, home improvements) based on contraceptive use.
- The scheme has reduced the impact of AIDS, but some say it has damaged the tourist industry.

21 For example in Qatar:

In 2000, a nationalisation policy was put in place. In a bid to curb the rising population imbalance (1.66 men for every woman, 2.46 men in the working age groups), a Permanent Population Committee was set up tasked with drafting a national strategy that focuses on achieving sustainable development with regard to population issues. The government has implemented a policy the aim of which is to try to reduce the percentage of foreign workers in the workforce, which in 2000 stood at 86%. This so far has not been hugely effective. However, the 2009 recession has had an impact on the numbers of people migrating to the country as many building projects ground to a halt, and rents increased. By the end of 2009, the country was showing a negative net migration rate.

22 Consequences could range from a loss of services, including, for example, the post office or general store; loss of the younger population by migration; areas falling into disrepair. It is better if you can illustrate each of these points with reference to a real location that you have studied or know.

23 Consequences include changes in the age structure of the area and in the socioeconomic status of the area — more affluent people, more car ownership, increased house prices and a change in the nature of services (e.g. types of shops, and eating houses) in the community. It is better if you can illustrate each of these points with reference to a real location that you have studied or know.

24 The precise detail will depend upon the example chosen, but some common elements may be seen. Although population growth has slowed down in the last 30 years, there is an increasing demand for housing — social changes such as separation and divorce have all led to a need for further housing development. There is an increasing number of elderly and a reduction in the number of children; smaller

family size; growth in single person households – both for elderly (mostly female) and young adults (mainly males).

This has contributed to continued expansion on the urban fringe — detached, executive-style housing, despite smaller families. There has been the growth of housing in regeneration schemes, conversion of former industrial units or commercial units, the 'docklands' type of development, more flats and apartments. There has been the growth in 'starter homes' and single occupancy units, and in houses and homes adapted for elderly residents, flats and modern terraced homes (generally up to two bedroom) mainly in central (brownfield) locations.

25 Note this question asks for contrasts, i.e. differences. The contrasts should come in the context of a range of characteristics: housing type, ethnicity, age structure, wealth, employment and the provision of services. Much of this material can be obtained from the census (if UK-based). Note that the information should be at a local scale — if you are using the census, then access materials at Lower Super Output Area (LSOA) level or ward level.

26 In 1981, the ethnic population is, in percentage terms, concentrated in the inner wards, particularly to the north of the city centre (5 and 11). The higher densities > 10% were found in a belt running north–south just east of centre line (7–8 south to 11–13). Much lower percentages are found on the periphery to the west and even in inner areas to the west of city centre. By 2001, there is some modification to the pattern, although the highest concentration, in the same classes, is still found in central, inner northern wards 5 and 11. The belt (> 10%) from 7–8 southwards has been extended right across the city to 3–9 on the southern edge. Ward 14 now has > 10% concentration. There is now > 5% ethnic concentration in all wards to the east of the city centre and in inner wards to the west. The areas on the western periphery (1–15) have < 5% concentration. The Asian and black ethnic population has maintained a strong concentration in the central areas, but there are clear indications of dispersal to outer areas in the last 20 years. The pattern has changed to some extent; it was already well established in the central wards by 1981.

27 For this type of question you should refer to the settlement case studies (inner city, suburban area, rural–urban fringe and rural settlement) you have studied. You should give place-specific detail.

There may be areas where there are concentrations of elderly people (sheltered accommodation, care homes or bungalows); young wealthy adults (regenerated areas of an inner city); student areas (low-cost flat areas); areas where families are more common.

Similarly there will be areas of low average incomes (old inner-city areas, high-rise flats, peripheral council estates, Housing Association properties) and areas with higher than average incomes (private housing estates, gated communities, exclusive apartments).

28 Social welfare refers to the factors that affect the ways in which people lead their lives on a daily basis, and covers areas such as housing (including domestic energy costs), shopping, education, health, access to leisure facilities, employment and transport.

29 High unemployment in an area may impact on the provision of services and other facilities. For example, low-price retail outlets may dominate; there is some evidence to suggest that supermarkets avoid such areas and as a result the quality of food for sale is both lower in quality and less varied, and there is a greater incidence of fast food outlets — giving rise to 'food deserts'. Schools tend to have lower rates of examination success; there are more schools in special measures, and/or are areas where a new 'Academy' can be found. On the other hand, there is evidence that such areas have greater healthcare provision — do Primary Care Trusts reflect areas of greater need in their provision? Housing quality in areas of high unemployment is lower than average. It is often badly maintained and, due to poor energy conservation, gives rise to high energy costs.

30 Population change may result from either natural factors or migration. Similarly, the consequences can be seen as either positive or negative. A high-level response will make good use of examples and case studies. Some general points may include:
- **Population increase — economic:** unemployment; pressure on resources such as food, housing, health and schools may be considered. There may be reference to the need to provide for an ageing or a young dependent population. Conversely, an increase in population may stimulate economic growth and lead to jobs being filled, possibly unwanted jobs or those demanding certain skills; more money paid in taxes; a rise in public spending.

- **Population decrease — economic:** stagnation of the economy — loss of young migrants, less money paid in taxes, loss of skills but some money sent back by migrants
- **Population increase — political:** the need to allocate resources; may refer to the need to increase food production, increase taxation to fund health-care of elderly; the need to introduce population policies regarding reducing birth rates or migration
- **Population decrease — political:** policies to encourage natural increase, or immigration, in order to stem the outflow of population, or to develop resources
- **Commentary** is likely to refer to the relative importance of economic and political impacts; whether effects are negative or positive or the severity of one particular aspect; or perceived knock-on effects. Any view expressed that can be supported by the evidence will be credited.

Food supply issues

1 Agricultural production has risen faster than the population since 1961. In fact, it has been doing so by a widening margin. In the last year or so of this period there is a sign that the gap may be closing. Production per head, however, has grown at a much slower rate.

2 Global trade in agricultural products has grown in the period in question but only at about the rate of global economic output. The trade has not grown faster because:
- agricultural tariffs have remained high (unlike tariffs on industrial goods)
- developed countries have support policies on their domestic agriculture which limits market penetration from outside
- developing countries have often followed a policy of import substitution
- the developed countries were not able to absorb much of the production coming from developing countries (e.g. tea, coffee and cocoa)

3 Fair Trade agreements mean that producers in the developing world sell their commodities to companies in the developed world at a rate above market price. This extra money is used to provide a better standard of living for the producers. Prominent Fair Trade goods are coffee, nuts, bananas and tea.

4 This is when developed countries export food and sell it in developing countries at very low prices in order to create markets in those areas. The developed countries therefore get rid of agricultural surpluses, but over-dependence on imports may be the result in developing countries. It is not unknown for dumping to occur between developed countries.

5 Subsistence agriculture is where a plot of land produces only enough food to feed the family working it or the local group (tribe etc.), pay taxes and sometimes leave a little surplus for barter or sale in better years. The main priority of working the land is self-sufficiency. Farmers tend to grow as wide a range of crops as is possible. Animals are often kept, but it is rare for them to be allowed to graze or fodder crops grown for their consumption. The only exception to this is the tribes of pastoral nomads who move around the semi-arid areas of the world.

6 This is extensive grain farming. It takes place on the vast expanses of the world's temperate grasslands, such as the steppes in Russia and the prairies of North America. Such vast areas have a huge amount of fairly flat land which is ideal for the machinery shown in the photograph (combine harvesters).

7 This is a package of agricultural improvements seen as the answer to the food problems in many parts of the less developed world. The basis of the Green Revolution was the introduction of high-yielding varieties of seeds, particularly of rice, wheat, maize, sorghum and millet. With the exception of rice, all the new seeds were drought resistant. They were all also responsive to fertilisers and had a shorter growing season. In the growing of rice, this allowed three crops a year to be obtained from the same land rather than the two of previous years.

8 Some of the benefits of the Green Revolution are:
- yields are two to four times greater than with traditional varieties
- three crops may be grown per year instead of two
- farm incomes have increased allowing the purchase of some machinery, better seeds and fertilisers
- the diet of rural communities is now more varied
- employment has been created in industries supplying inputs to farms

9 Some of the disadvantages of using HYV seeds are:
- high inputs of fertiliser are required to optimise production

- much greater use of pesticides with the consequent environmental impact
- rural debt can rise as farmers borrow money to pay for the inputs
- more weed control is required and the seeds are often more susceptible to pests and diseases
- middle- and high-income farmers have benefited more than those on low incomes, thus widening the income gap in rural communities
- many claim that crops grown from HYVs have an inferior flavour
- with the possible increase in irrigation, salinisation can increase
- greater dependence of countries on the TNCs that provide seeds, fertilisers, pesticides and machinery

10 Genetic modification involves taking some of the DNA from one species and placing it in the DNA of another species. When this happens, one or more characteristics of the donor species are transferred to the new plant. For example, adding the gene from a plant that grows well in a semi-arid environment to rice DNA can extend rice growing into drier areas. Many people claim that this could solve food shortages throughout the world and reduce the inputs of chemicals into farming.

11 Critics of the genetic modification of crops are concerned that pollen from GM plants may pollinate nearby standard plants and that this may spread the modifications in an uncontrolled way. Objectors are also concerned that the long-term effects of GM crops on human health are unknown.

12 This is a pest control strategy that uses an array of complementary methods: natural predators and parasites, pest-resistant varieties, cultural practices and biological controls. Pesticides are used only as a last resort.

13 Hormones are used in farm animals to stimulate growth by increasing the efficiency at which feed is converted to muscle. Beef animals produce less fat and, therefore, leaner meat for consumers. Other hormones are used to increase milk yields from dairy cattle. Some authorities are concerned that hormone residue in meat and milk might be harmful to human health and to the environment. It has been questioned whether such hormones could disrupt human hormone balance causing development problems, interfering with the reproductive system and even leading to the development of breast, colon or prostate cancer. Scientists are also concerned that hormone residues may enter various natural environments and have a substantial effect on reproductive capacity.

14 Appropriate technology is the use of small-scale, sustainable, low-tech ideas that are appropriate to the local climate and environment, and to the wealth, skills and needs of the local population.

15 In Burkina Faso, which lies in the Sahel, it is important to be able to conserve the limited water that is available. One conservation method in widespread use is the construction across fields of **contour stone lines (bunds)**, which slow down and filter runoff thereby increasing infiltration and controlling soil erosion by capturing sediment.

16 Large areas of Amazonia have been deforested in order to provide pasture and land for growing soya beans. Brazil is now a leading producer of grains, which accounts for more than one-third of the country's GDP. Increasing the cultivated area is a way of increasing agricultural production to meet the demands of a rapidly growing population.

17 Land reform is the redistribution of land and it can be used to overcome the inefficiencies in the use of land and labour. One aspect of land reform is the appropriation of large estates by a government and redistributing that land to landless people or communal groups.

18 The Common Agricultural Policy is the way in which agriculture is organised in the EU. The CAP was set up in 1960 with the following aims:
- to increase agricultural production within the area
- to ensure a fair standard of living for farmers
- to stabilise agricultural markets within and between members
- to ensure reasonable consumer prices
- to maintain employment in agricultural areas

19 Quotas are used to restrict trade of a particular commodity between countries. A country fixes a figure and import above that figure is not allowed. For example, the EU put quotas on banana imports from certain Latin American countries, in order to favour imports from areas such as the West Indies. These countries protested to the World Trade Organization (WTO) and the EU had to back down and open its markets fully to Latin American producers.

20 The reason that governments give farmers subsidies is to encourage them to grow certain crops in order to maintain home-grown supplies.

21 Because of subsidies, interventionist prices and import tariffs on foreign produce many farmers do not have to face a competitive market. When they were guaranteed to sell all they could produce many farmers produced too much and this created surpluses in certain products, particularly cereals, butter, beef, apples, oranges, tobacco and wine. These huge surpluses became known as 'mountains' and 'lakes'.

22 Set aside was a policy of the CAP directed mainly at the overproduction of cereals. Established originally on a voluntary basis, farmers were paid to take land out of production and put it to grass, woodland or some non-agricultural use. As cereals continued to be overproduced, the EU forced farmers who were receiving subsidies to take 15% of their land out of production. Most governments agreed that set aside works quickly and provides environmental benefits. With reduced cereal harvests in the 2000s, the EU has had to review this policy and in 2009 it announced that compulsory set aside was at an end for the foreseeable future. In the UK, farmers can still volunteer to set aside some of their land, particularly for environmental gains.

23 Environmental stewardship is where farmers are paid to deliver simple but effective management of the environment. Farmers can choose from over 50 options, including stone wall maintenance, creating buffer strips, hedgerow management, ditch and pond management, infield tree protection, rush pasture management, stubble control, archaeological site management, and bird and flower conservation. Organic farmers are encouraged to join as DEFRA recognises that they may be able to deliver greater environmental benefits.

24 Buffer zones are areas along field boundaries, around ponds and along ditches which the farmer does not plant. Benefits include:
- habitats for small mammals and birds are preserved and new ones created
- habitats are protected from pesticides and fertilisers
- banks can be stabilised
- water courses are protected from pollution

25 From Figure 1.29 the following can be observed and comment made:

- Transport by HGV is by far the biggest source of air pollution. It accounts for well over half of all emissions.
- Over 75% of emissions come from road transport.
- Over 10% of emissions come from sea transport.
- This is nearly matched by air transport, which in some ways is a surprise, but not if you look at the amount of food in UK supermarkets that could be air-freighted into the country.
- Quite a large amount of emissions come from cars, presumably in taking food from the shop/supermarket to the home.

26 In organic farming, food is grown or reared and processed according to certain rules. These include: using natural fertilisers that build up the organic content of the soil; not using herbicides or pesticides (some very restricted use of pesticides is permitted); not confining animals and allowing access to pasture; usually carrying out crop rotation to stop pests and diseases building up from season to season.

Figure 1.30 shows that there was substantial increase in the number of organic farms in the UK from 1997 up to 2001. Numbers went from under 1000 to around 4000 in those 4 years. Since then numbers have stabilised around that figure with small drops occurring in some years. The peak number appears to be in 2003 when there were over 4000 organic farms in the UK.

27 The benefits of having more local produce on sale include:
- fresher produce in the shops
- local economy boosted by the support of local food producers
- boosting local economy in this way might start a multiplier effect
- promotion of local diversity

28 An agribusiness is a large business involved in some aspect of agricultural production. This includes farming, contract farming, seeds, agrichemicals, machinery, distribution, processing and marketing. Some companies even extend into retail sales. A small number of agribusinesses now dominate each part of the food chain in developed countries.

29 Critics are unhappy with the amount of power that these companies wield and their influence on governments and international organisations such as the WTO. Points (not always substantiated) made against them include:

- the global nature of their businesses gives them a political voice in a number of countries — a voice that reflects their interests
- allocating labour-intensive processes to low-wage economies
- carrying out environmentally damaging processes in countries with lenient environmental regulations
- their operations have led to the destruction of traditional agricultural practices
- many commodities produced in developing countries are not directed at local needs
- some agribusinesses have been at the forefront of the promotion and use of GM crops

30 Sustainable agriculture is defined as the ability of a farmer to produce food indefinitely without causing irreversible damage to the local ecosystem. Sustainable practice replaces nutrients in the soil while minimising the use of non-renewable resources and trying to avoid the use of chemicals that could damage the environment.

Energy issues

1 **Flow resources** (also known as renewable resources) have a natural rate of availability. They yield a continuous flow that can be consumed in any given time period without endangering future consumption, as long as current use does not exceed net renewal during the same period. **Stock resources** (also known as non-renewable resources) are those that have been built up, or have evolved, over geological time. They cannot be used without depleting the stock because their rate of formation is so slow as to be meaningless in terms of the human life span.

2 **Primary energy** is that which can be used in its natural form to produce heat and power. It includes fossil fuels such as coal and oil, renewable energy such as solar and wind and also sources such as fuelwood and biomass. **Secondary energy** is that which is produced or made, derived from a primary source. Electricity and petrol come into this category.

3 There has been a reduction in the use of coal and, to a lesser extent, oil. Natural gas has become much more important, and is now the UK's single largest contributor to electricity generation. Nuclear power has shown a slight increase as has renewable energy, especially wind power. However, the proportion from renewable sources is still low at less than 10%.

4 Trends in the consumption of all fuels have risen and are likely to continue to rise. This is due to the continued economic growth not only of the established economic powers in the world — USA, Japan, EU — but also of the emerging economies of China, India and Brazil. The largest increase will be in the use of coal — caused by industrial growth in China where there are huge reserves of coal. This goes against the requirement to cut greenhouse gases in order to reduce global warming. Fossil fuels will continue to dominate world energy consumption. The largest renewable source is biomass; all renewable sources show modest increases.

5 Highest production is in North America and northern Europe (UK, Norway and Russia). There are also high rates of supply in the Middle East (oil). Africa (except Libya and Angola) and Asia have low rates of energy production, as does South America (with the exception of Venezuela).

6 Highest consumption rates tend to occur in similar areas to supply – North America, Russia, Saudi Arabia and Turkmenistan. Areas with high consumption also include parts of Europe, Argentina and Australia. Africa and China/India have low rates of energy consumption. High consumption is associated with extremes of temperatures — cold areas require heat, and hot areas require air conditioning, and desalination plants for water. Extensive unpopulated land areas such as Argentina and Australia give rise to greater vehicle fuel consumption.

7 There is major movement of oil from the Middle East. Supplies radiate from here to all parts of the world — over 900 million tonnes move from the area each year. The USA is a major receiver of oil; it imports over 600 million tonnes. Western Europe is another large net importer — again over 600 million tonnes. Other large importers of oil include Japan (over 200 million tonnes) and China (160 million tonnes). Russia is a large exporter of oil — over 380 million tonnes.

8 OPEC is the Organization of Petroleum Exporting Countries. It is the name of the cartel that sets output quotas in order to control crude oil prices. In the 1970s, OPEC had great power when it controlled 90% of the world's supply of crude oil exports. Its influence, however, has been reduced (36% of world production in 2008), as the higher price of oil allowed more expensive fields, such as the North Sea and Alaska, to be brought into production. The headquarters of OPEC are in Vienna.

Answers

The members of OPEC are Algeria, Nigeria, Angola, Qatar, Iran, Saudi Arabia, Iraq, United Arab Emirates, Kuwait, Venezuela, Libya and Ecuador.

Indonesia was suspended from membership in 2008 when it became a net importer of oil, which reduced the membership to 12 countries.

9 This can be approached in a number of ways:
- the role of trading groups such OPEC, where prices are fixed within a range
- the increasing cost of oil and its impact on the economies of rich countries and implications for poorer countries
- the impact traders in international stock markets have on fuel prices
- pressure placed on countries to increase production and reduce prices
- the extent to which countries use their energy resources as a source of political power, e.g. Russia and the supply of natural gas
- the impact of sanctions and other restrictions, e.g. Iraq in the recent past, and Iran more recently

10 Natural gas is transported in two main ways:
- by pipeline, for example across extensive areas of Russia and eastern Europe
- as LNG (liquefied natural gas) — for example, a LNG terminal supplying natural gas to the UK has opened recently at Milford Haven in South Wales

11 There are a number of environmental impacts that could be referred to:
- Acid rain: impact of rainfall with a higher level of acidity on forests, soils, rivers, lakes and buildings. Causes are the pollutants sulphur dioxide and nitrogen oxides from power stations that use fossil fuels, and pollutants from vehicle exhausts.
- Areas of exploitation: open-cast mining, and surface removal of oil tars from shales; unsightly spoil heaps from underground mining; potential spillages of oil from pipelines.
- Global warming could also be referred to, even though it is not on the AS specification. It is caused by the release of carbon dioxide from burning fossil fuels in power stations, and by other greenhouse gas emissions (e.g. from cattle ranching and indirectly from deforestation).
- Photochemical smog is a consequence of the use of petrol and diesel.

12 a Solar electricity is currently produced in two ways:
- Photovoltaic systems can operate anywhere where there is sunlight of any intensity. Panels made of different materials, such as glass and plastic, can be used. Entire roofs can be covered in this way.
- Concentrated systems use mirrors, lenses and tracking systems to focus a large area of sunlight into a small beam. This concentrated light is then used as a heat source in a conventional power station. Areas where this takes place include Spain, California and Australia.

b Wind power requires access to the wind where it is both frequent and strong. Open, exposed hills and coastal areas are suitable sites. The Pennines and off the east and west coasts of the UK have seen the development of wind farms. Wind farms provoke debate, so sites where there will be minimal objection are also favoured.

13 TNCs such as BP, Shell and Exxon play a significant role in the identification of oil reserves and their subsequent extraction. They have access to the technologies and information required to enable both of these processes. They try to recruit local people in the extraction process and often provide training programmes for them. They also have their own pipelines and ships to transport oil and gas around the world. They have their own refineries at the point of importation, producing a wide range of fuels and lubricants. They also have large numbers of retail outlets where oils and petrol are sold to the general public. In many ways they dominate the production and distribution of oil and its derivatives.

14 Although the UK has large reserves of coal (some say they could last for 300 years), they are not considered to be economically viable compared with the cost of other fuels and imported coal.

Clean air legislation within the UK has led to an increase in demand for cleaner, less polluting forms of fuel.

Pressure to reduce carbon emissions that cause global warming has made coal power even more unpopular with both environmentalists and governments.

15 Gas-fired power stations will produce more of the UK's electricity, but the origin of the gas being burnt will change from being home-produced gas to imported gas. The imported gas will come from countries such as Norway and possibly Russia, and much of it will arrive in ships as LNG. This will require the development of specialist ports. Nuclear power will decrease in the short term as stations

deemed to be outdated are decommissioned. The power stations are being decommissioned in phases, with the last one, Sizewell A, closing after 2025. Although they are being decommissioned, they will still be dangerous for some time afterwards. There are plans to build more new nuclear power stations to replace those that have been closed.

16 Environmental problems are concerned with the rapid rate at which trees are being cut down as populations grow. This will impact on the hydrological cycle with less interception, greater exposure of the ground surface and greater surface runoff. Therefore, the likelihood of flooding and soil erosion will increase. In hot arid areas, the risk of desertification will increase.

17 Biomass refers to living and decaying organic matter. Fuelwood can be used to produce energy, as with cut-down vegetation in the Sahel. Crop residues and dung can be burnt for cooking purposes. Modern biofuels are produced from plantations of designated vegetation, such as sugar cane for ethanol in Brazil, and *Miscanthus* and willow in the UK, which are converted to a gas for burning at power stations.

18 Compared with other forms of fuel, only small amounts of uranium are needed to produce a given output of heat. This must be seen in the context of world energy needs; it is unlikely that demand can be met from renewable sources and yet other sources such as coal, oil and gas are finite. There is no shortage of uranium and operating costs are very competitive. Although there are questions of safety and environmental damage, so far nuclear plants have a good record in relation to other forms of electricity production and they produce less carbon dioxide and sulphur dioxide.

19 In terms of development, wave power is still in its infancy. It involves using the power of the waves to generate electricity, either through the weight of the water itself or by pushing air through turbines. One scheme in Portugal involved Pelamis machines, developed by a Scottish company, which were a series of red tubes, each about the size of a small commuter train, linked together, and pointed in the direction of the waves. The waves travelled down the tubes, causing them to bob up and down, and a hydraulic system harnessed this movement to generate electricity.

Tidal power is also a renewable method of producing energy by using the movements of the tide. With reversible blades, schemes could harness both the incoming and outgoing tides and, therefore, maximise the use of the site. Places with the maximum tidal range offer the greatest potential. The major drawback is cost, in both economic and environmental terms, and this may explain why only two sites are at present in operation: the Rance Estuary in northwest France and on the Bay of Fundy in eastern Canada.

20 Applications for wind farms have increased during this time period, with a small fall in 2006. However, the percentage of successful applications has fallen from 75% to 66%. In 2005, only half the applications were successful. This could be due to local people objecting to having wind farms in their areas because they deem them to be unsightly and noisy. It is clear that not all people view wind farms as being desirable.

21 Types of energy that come under the heading 'appropriate technology' are most suitable for developing countries. This means the use of technical expertise and equipment that are suited to the economic and technological development of the country involved. These could include the use of micro-hydro schemes using 'run of the river' systems where the water from a river is diverted into a turbine, and biogas schemes using methane gas produced from fermentation pits containing cow dung and decaying organic matter.

22 The Kyoto Protocol was the outcome of a meeting in 1997 at which over 100 governments signed a 'Climate Change Protocol'. This set specific legally binding targets for pollution mitigation and proposed schemes to enable governments to reach these targets. The goal of the Kyoto Protocol was to reduce worldwide greenhouse gas emissions to 5.2% below 1990 levels between 2008 and 2012. Compared with the emission levels that would occur by 2010 without the Kyoto Protocol, this target represented a 29% cut. It is due to expire in 2012. In December 2009, a conference took place in Copenhagen with the aim of replacing the Kyoto Protocol. Unfortunately, the countries that attended failed to agree a further legally binding agreement to reduce carbon emissions. They did agree that there is a need to limit global temperatures rising by no more than 2°C above pre-industrial levels.

23 A number of ways of energy conservation are shown:
- triple-glazed windows to retain heat in the building
- small wind turbine to augment the mains electricity supply
- house built facing south so that heat from the sun can be utilised
- green roof to act as an insulator, preventing heat loss
- reusing raw materials for housing materials so that energy is not used in their production elsewhere

24 They could:
- encourage car sharing schemes
- give incentives to encourage people to work from home
- have systems of regular energy monitoring — switching off lights, or using photocells and timers, and regulating heating
- organise energy-awareness campaigns, and appoint energy coordinators

25 A wide range of transport policies could be examined here:
- improving public transport systems — park-and-ride schemes, electric tram systems, quality bus corridors
- reduced tax on some fuels — LPG and biodiesels
- varying vehicle excise duty according to the size of the vehicle, the type of fuel used and the level of carbon dioxide emissions produced
- congestion charge discounts or supplements depending on the type of vehicle
- increasing the price of car parking in urban centres
- introducing a low-emission zone where users of heavily polluting vehicles are charged

26 Nuclear power provokes a negative environmental image with past disasters such as Chernobyl and Three Mile Island. There is also the need to dispose of nuclear waste safely because it remains radioactive for many years. The burying of this waste in deep and sound geological formations is the current proposed solution. However, no sites have yet been identified and people are likely to resist moves to have it happening near them. Much nuclear waste in the UK is currently stored above ground in safe storage at Sellafield. There are risks involved in the transportation of nuclear waste to the storage site, as well as dangers of leakages into the atmosphere, sea and groundwater supplies. Health risks are often stated and some people cite the risk of terrorist attacks.

27 Some people state that as the population and demand for energy increases, supplies of finite resources will decrease. As industrialisation occurs around the world, this will itself cause a greater demand for energy. More energy will be needed by the increasingly affluent population created by industrialisation. There will be more demand for vehicle and air transport, both of which consume fuel derived from oil. There is a limit to the amount of new oil reserves that can be found on the planet.

28 There are six major oil TNCs, most of which operate under a variety of names. The only company to retain its name throughout the world is Shell, a UK/Dutch company. It would seem that all the companies seek to have a North American identity and a European identity; Chevron is the only player that has a Central/South American identity. Total, a French company, operates under two names within Europe, and nowhere else. The purpose of having a variety of names is to widen the market share, and may be due to previous takeovers.

29 France's energy mix is as follows:
- nuclear: 74.5%
- hydroelectric: 16.2%
- thermal: 9.2%
- wind power and other renewable sources: 0.1%

In Iceland, renewable energy supplies 89% of Iceland's primary energy needs, mainly in the form of HEP. Of the 11% of Iceland's electricity that is not currently generated from renewable sources, 1% is generated from imported oil, gas, fossil fuel and wood power — virtually all the remainder comes from geothermal power. Geothermal sources are also used to heat 89% of the buildings in Iceland, with the remaining being heated with electricity.

30 This could be answered in a general sense as well with reference to two countries or areas. For example, you could refer to the use of renewable energy sources versus continuing to use non-renewable sources. Alternatively, you could refer to the use of appropriate technology. Another approach could be to focus on energy conservation versus energy production.

For renewable energy sources, advantages could include sustainability, longevity, environmentally friendly. Disadvantages could include expensive technology, varying efficiency, perceived negative impact on the environment (e.g. wind power). Non-renewable resources are available and relatively cheap and easy to extract. However, they raise environmental issues (this would need developing) and are not sustainable.

Health issues

1 **Morbidity** relates to experiencing illness or disease. It has a consequential effect on quality of life, reducing it. Many illnesses have a debilitating effect, but do not lead to death. Morbidity is measured by DALYs (Disability Adjusted Life Years lost) — the number of healthy years lost through illness. **Mortality** refers to death. There are various indicators used: crude death rate, infant mortality rate, maternal mortality rate.

2 **Maternal mortality** is the number of mothers who die for every 100 000 live births per year. In 2007, the maternal mortality ratio was nine in developed countries, 450 in developing countries and 900 in sub-Saharan Africa. This means that 99% of the women who die in pregnancy and childbirth are from the developing countries. Slightly more than half of these deaths occurred in sub-Saharan Africa and about a third in southern Asia; together these two regions accounted for over 85% of maternal deaths worldwide.

3 The disease could be chosen from a wide range — cancers, heart disease, strokes, type 2 diabetes and obesity. There should be reference to areas where the incidence is high and areas where the incidence is low. It would be good to provide examples of anomalies where individual countries or groups of countries go against these trends.

4 Cholera is essentially a disease of the tropics, with much of sub-Saharan Africa having cases. Cholera also features in southwest Asia, and in southeast and southern Asia. The rest of the developed world tends to only have imported cases, i.e. people with the disease have entered the country. There are some interesting anomalies: the USA has its own cases, and there are also countries in Africa and Asia (e.g. Botswana and Pakistan) where the disease does not apparently exist. Could it be that the disease is not reported here?

5 The response will depend on the disease studied. Impacts should refer to the effect of ill-health, reduced life expectancy, access to treatment, inability to work and provide for the family, and the impact this will have on other family members. You could

also refer to the need to depend on other members of the extended family or on the state. Issues associated with discrimination and attitudes to illness could also be relevant.

6 Three ways in which an infectious disease can be prevented or managed are:
   - development of a vaccine (such as for AIDS) — this has a direct link to the economic development of a country
   - changing the way in which people live in an area where the disease exists — for example using insecticide-treated anti-malaria nets at night (a change in the lifestyle of people)
   - prolonging the life of people by using drugs (as with AIDS) — improving the health of people

7 The number of people living with HIV has increased fourfold between 1990 and 2007, although the rate of increase appears to be slowing. This is supported by the fact that the number of newly infected people is falling, and has continued to fall since 1996. This could be due to greater awareness of the condition and how to prevent it. The number of deaths from AIDS rose continuously until 2005, but now appears to be falling. This could be due to the effectiveness of anti-retroviral drugs such as AZT and HAART.

8 The response will depend on the disease studied. Statements should include the loss of earnings to the individual and tax revenues to the state, long-term sickness and the inability to support oneself and family, the need to give up work and rely on benefits and/or pension. At a national level, there is the need to provide healthcare, and the need to fund research and development for new drugs/care strategies, all of which has to be paid for. However, this also provides employment and wealth-earning opportunities.

9 This answer uses type 2 diabetes as the example. Around the world, 90% of people with diabetes have type 2 diabetes. It is largely the result of excess body weight and physical inactivity. Over time, diabetes can damage the heart, blood vessels, eyes, kidneys and nerves. Diabetes is a cause of blindness, and occurs as a result of long-term accumulated damage to the small blood vessels in the retina. After 15 years of diabetes, approximately 2% of people become blind and about 10% develop severe visual impairment. Diabetic neuropathy is damage to the nerves as a result of diabetes and affects up to 50% of people with the disease. Combined with reduced blood flow, neuropathy in the feet increases the

chance of foot ulcers and eventual limb amputation. Diabetes is among the leading causes of kidney failure — 10–20% of people with diabetes die of kidney failure. Diabetes also increases the risk of heart disease and stroke. The overall risk of dying among people with diabetes is at least double the risk of their peers without diabetes.

10 **Malnutrition** is a condition resulting from some form of dietary deficiency. This may be because the quantity of food (measured in calories per day) is too low or because certain important food nutrients, such as vitamins, are absent. Malnutrition weakens the immune system and makes people more vulnerable to diseases. It may also lead to deficiency diseases such as beriberi or anaemia. **Undernourishment** is the condition that results from consuming too little food over a period of time.

11 Two physical causes of periodic famine are:
- **drought**: lack of rainfall causes soil and underground sources of water to decline. This results in a soil-moisture deficit and hence the usual growth of crops and grazing grounds cannot be maintained.
- **severe flooding** : washes away and/or destroys vital food supplies, especially if it occurs close to harvest.

12 Two human causes of periodic famine are:
- a population increase greater than the rate of food production — this may occur in areas where there is a sudden influx of refugees, fleeing a war zone or an area of civil unrest. It can also occur as people migrate from one drought zone to another.
- a rapid rise in the price of foodstuffs and/or animals — this can occur when the quality of farmland and grazing land declines (often during a drought). It is further compounded by a breakdown in the local economy and marketing systems. Control mechanisms react too slowly and inflationary price rises fuel panic buying, which leads rapidly to shortages of basic foodstuffs.

13 The example taken is drought in southern Ethiopia and Somalia, 2000.

In 2000, the rains failed, leading to a severe drought that affected a large proportion of the population. The drought had the following effects:
- It led to unusual movements of people and livestock as herders moved in search of water and fresh pasture, which put pressure on those areas that had sufficient water and pasture.
- The lack of food and water took a heavy toll on herders and thousands of cattle, sheep, camels and goats died.
- The death of livestock led to a deterioration in people's nutritional status.
- Milk, one of the main components of the diet (particularly that of women and children) became scarce.
- Food prices began to rise.
- Thousands of families abandoned their lands and headed for the large towns. Many camps for these internally displaced persons had to be set up, housing thousands of people.
- Large amounts of foreign aid were required to run these camps.

14 A longer-term response to famine prevention involves helping people develop a more productive system of farming. Such aid could involve:
- increased use of fertilisers and new technologies such as high-yielding varieties of seeds to encourage the production of more food
- improvements to transport and communication systems to ensure that produce gets to markets more efficiently
- easing international trade and cancelling national debt

15 The information shows that the proportion of overweight people (including obese) increases with age until 55–64 years for men and 65–74 years for women, when it then declines. There is consistently a higher proportion of overweight men than women, with the gap being widest from 35 to 54 years. Only in the youngest adult age group is the percentage of overweight people less than 40%.

16 The impact of obesity relates to the onset and likelihood of other illnesses such as heart disease, strokes, type 2 diabetes, certain cancers, impacts and stresses on joints such as hips, and osteoarthritis. Strategies include increased health education concerning healthy diets and lifestyles, encouraging access to sports facilities and exercise, and encouragement of walking and cycling to school. They also include marketing strategies by manufacturers and retailers to offer healthy options, school dinner initiatives, and other preventative measures.

17 A National Health Service is a state-supported and operated service. The system is financed by national government taxation (the national insurance scheme in the UK) and in Canada is supplemented by provincial government taxation. The facilities used are mainly publicly owned, although recently there have been moves to share with the private sector. Doctors and nurses are regulated by the state and by professional bodies, which set standards of care. Access is free to all, irrespective of income and need.

18 Cuba and the USA have totally different healthcare systems. The system in Cuba is socialist. It is a fully controlled state system financed by taxation whereas the US system is totally private (or pluralistic), financed by the individual through insurance payments. (Note: President Obama is trying to modify this.) The outcomes in terms of infant mortality rate and life expectancy are little different. You could comment on the relative cost effectiveness. In addition, Cuba has had to address related issues such as education, nutrition, distribution of wealth and sanitation. It could be argued that healthcare is as much a function of social care as it is of medical care.

19 Clear references must be made to the two chosen countries. It is likely that one will be a developed country and the other a developing country. The contrasts may relate to sources of funding, the arrangements for monitoring provision, the balance between state and private care, the role of professional associations and remuneration.

20 TNCs are involved in research to develop drugs to act either as cures or to offset the effects of diseases. There are issues as to which diseases have most investment and whether these are the ones with most need. However, need varies around the world and there is the parallel issue of recouping investment. Production and sale of drugs also give rise to issues — such as whether they are sold under a brand name or a generic name. The latter are sold at much cheaper prices. Profit is a key aspect of TNC drug development. There are issues associated with distribution and marketing — directly to doctors in some cases, rather than through government agencies. Some people believe that TNCs target symptoms rather than causes.

21 The high cost of research and development means that pharmaceutical companies can only continue developing new drugs if they are able to recoup their costs when they sell these drugs. The industry spends approximately $500 million to research a new drug. With the profits made, the pharmaceutical industry has taken on a number of philanthropic (charitable) initiatives in recent years, such as lowering the cost of AIDS drugs to about $1000 per person per year in some cases and distributing free drugs to treat diseases such as river blindness and malaria. Another problem is that many drugs do not reach the people that need them. The distribution of drugs is a problem that has a number of deep-seated causes — political instability, bureaucracy, poor health infrastructure, corruption and other education and social obstacles — and these all add to costs.

22 Smoking is increasing in certain parts of the developing world, particularly in India and China. This will lead to an increase in non-communicable diseases (circulatory diseases and cancers) in these areas. On the other hand, if taxed, the industry will contribute large amounts to state funds, which could be ploughed into healthcare provision. In addition, large numbers of people are employed by the industry.

23 Very few countries have complete policies on any aspect of tobacco control, the largest being 20 countries that have complete advertising bans. Only 84 countries have any form of policy on smoke-free environments, although the majority of countries have programmes for smoking cessation, and advertising bans. These types of policy are probably the least controversial because they place responsibility on the smoker. Surprisingly then only half of the countries place health warnings on packets. Over half of the countries use taxation as a policy — although this could be seen as a revenue provider.

24 Note that this question refers to 'regional' variations, so variations within an urban area are not acceptable. Descriptions should refer to the location of relatively high incidence of ill health, as well as low incidence, and variations in the types of disease. For example, there are higher rates of lung cancer in the north of England and Scotland due to higher rates of smoking. Scotland also has high rates of alcohol- and drug-related illnesses. On the other hand, London has the highest rates of infectious and respiratory diseases, which could be related to the multicultural nature of the area as it receives high numbers of immigrants. Reasoning could refer to income levels, education, lifestyle, age structure and variation in access to healthcare.

25 A Primary Care Trust (PCT) is a part of the UK National Health Service (NHS) that provides some primary care and community services or commissions them from other providers. PCTs are also involved in commissioning secondary care from the hospitals in its area. Many PCTs now call themselves NHS followed by the name of their geographical area to make it easier for local people to understand how the NHS is managed locally. Collectively, PCTs are responsible for spending around 80% of the total NHS budget.

26 It is important that you know what healthcare facilities exist in your local area. Your starting point should be the Health Profiles at **www.healthprofiles.info** where you can use a postcode to access healthcare needs in your area.

This will then provide you with the website of the local PCT where you can find out the names and types of local hospitals as well as information on GP services, opticians, dentists, pharmacies, maternal health facilities, mental health facilities and other health-related providers.

27 Charitable organisations offer support in a variety of situations not offered by the NHS. They also tend to concentrate on welfare as much as on health. Examples include:
- the Down's Syndrome Trust
- Macmillan cancer nurses
- the hospice movement
- organisations such as Shelter and Help the Aged

At an international scale, an example is Médecins Sans Frontières.

28 The Health Profile of the PCT in northern England is significantly worse than that of the PCT in eastern England. Nearly all the indicators in the northern PCT are significantly worse than the national average for England and one of the two not in this situation (adults who smoke) is still lower than the average for England. The northern PCT clearly has lots of health issues to address and there may be problems in terms of prioritising. On the other hand, the eastern England PCT is only significantly worse than the average for England for the physically active children indicator. For tooth decay in children, teenage pregnancy and adults who smoke it is significantly better than the average for England. This points to better education in this area, and/or a healthier attitude to lifestyle.

29 The following gives an indication of the type of local information that can be accessed. For one town in the UK:

On Monday and Tuesday evenings, the Staywell Clinic at Nobles hospital is run solely by women for women — the all female staff offer cervical screening, BMI measurements, blood pressure checks and breast examination advice. In addition, vaccinations against cervical cancer for all girls aged 13–18 commenced in April 2008. For men, testicular cancer awareness is high on the agenda and the Anti-Cancer Association runs a yearly programme of lectures for KS5 students in schools and colleges.

30 The response to a question such as this will depend on the area selected. Age may relate to provision for children and the need for prenatal and postnatal care. Equally, it could refer to provision for the elderly — flu jabs, residential homes and care for dementia patients. Gender could refer to the incidence of male-orientated industry-related diseases (such as in former coal mining areas) or the need to counsel young people regarding contraception. Wealth may impact on lifestyle provision, but could also link to aspects such as the lack of healthy diets in remote and deprived areas, and alcoholism (though this is not clear-cut). Wealth may have a significant link to access to exercise and good nutrition, though initiatives in the provision of school meals seek to counter this. Private exercise and fitness clubs tend to locate in areas where wealthy people can access them. Many council and housing association estates are remote from supermarkets, and low-income people have difficulty accessing them. This gives rise to the concept of 'food deserts' — areas where fast-food outlets dominate, with high-cost local food shops. Note that many of these elements are interrelated and a good answer will illustrate this.

Unit 3 Contemporary geographical issues

Plate tectonics and associated hazards

1 The **lithosphere** consists of the crust and the rigid upper section of the mantle. It is approximately 80–90 km thick. It is divided into seven large plates and a number of smaller ones. The **asthenosphere** is the semi-molten mass below the lithosphere on which the plates float and move.

2 The differences between the plates are shown in the following table.

	Continental crust	Oceanic crust
Thickness	30–70 km	6–10 km
Age	Over 1500 million years	Less than 200 million years
Density	2.6 (lighter)	3.0 (heavier)
Composition	Mainly granite; silicon, aluminium, oxygen (SIAL)	Mainly basalt; silicon, magnesium, oxygen (SIMA)

3 Wegener suggested originally that about 300 million years ago a single continent existed, which he called Pangaea. Later, he said, this super-continent split into two parts as continental drift moved sections apart from each other. This created two large continents, Laurasia to the north and Gondwanaland in the south.

His ideas failed to gain acceptance because he was unable to explain the mechanism that enabled the continents to drift apart.

4 The main evidence was:
- South America and Africa seemed to fit together.
- The glacial deposits of the late Carboniferous cover such a wide area now. They cannot be explained in this position, therefore the areas must have moved since the deposits were formed.
- Rock sequences in northern Scotland agree with some in eastern Canada, indicating that they were probably formed in the same area.
- Fossil remains of the reptile *Mesosaurus* are found in both South America and Africa. It is unlikely that this reptile could have developed in areas so wide apart.
- Fossil plants in coal are found in areas as wide apart today as India and Antarctica.

5 Sea-floor spreading is where the plates under the ocean are moving apart allowing magma to escape to the surface to form volcanoes and, on a grander scale, a mid-oceanic ridge. The best example lies down the middle of the Atlantic Ocean where the Eurasian and African plates are moving eastwards and the North and South American plates are moving west. Magma rising to the surface has formed a number of volcanic islands including Iceland. Down the middle of the ocean, the mid-Atlantic ridge has formed from the rising magma.

6 Either side of the mid-Atlantic ridge there are lavas in which the iron particles are aligned with Earth's magnetic field. At regular intervals the Earth's polarity reverses (approx. every 400 000 years). Therefore, lava that erupted in the past may have a different polarity from present-day lava. Either side of the ridge this produces a series of stripes, with the rocks aligned alternately between north and south poles. This indicates that the sea floor has moved away from its central position, with new sea floor forming behind it with a different polarity. The stripes are also older with distance from the central ridge (see diagram).

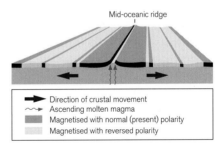

Mid-oceanic ridge

➤ Direction of crustal movement
〰 Ascending molten magma
▨ Magnetised with normal (present) polarity
▨ Magnetised with reversed polarity

7 As new crust forms and spreads away from the central ridge, transform faults occur at right angles to the plate boundary as parts of the plate move at different speeds. With the movement at different speeds friction results, which causes earthquakes to occur.

8 The following labels should be inserted on the diagram:

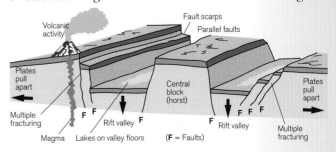

9 Subduction occurs when oceanic and continental plates meet. The oceanic plate is denser (3.0) than the continental (2.6) and is therefore forced under that plate. The downwarping of the oceanic plate forms a very deep part of the ocean known as a trench.

10 The following labels should be included on the diagram:

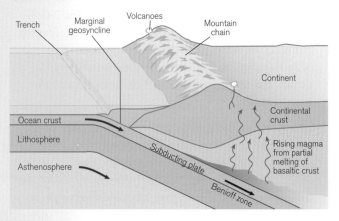

11 Continental plates have a much lower density than the underlying layers, therefore there is little subduction when they meet. As they move together, their edges and the sediments between them are forced up into fold mountains. With little subduction there is no volcanic activity, but plate movement can trigger shallow-focus earthquakes. As well as being forced up, material is forced downwards forming substantial roots for the fold mountains. The Indo-Australian plate meets the Eurasian plate north of India to form the Himalayan range of mountains that result from the sediments of the intervening Sea of Tethys being forced upwards. This uplift is still taking place today.

12 On conservative margins, two plates slide past each other with no destruction or creation of crust. As there is no subduction, volcanic activity does not occur. However, the movement produces a great deal of stress as the plates rub against each other creating friction. This triggers shallow-focus earthquakes. The best example is on the western side of North America where the Pacific and North American plates are moving parallel to each other in the same direction, but not at the same speed. The division between them is known as the San Andreas fault and is a noted earthquake zone.

13 Hot spots form where a concentration of radioactive elements develops in the mantle. From this, a plume of magma rises towards the surface and eats through the plate above. When this plume breaks through to the surface, active volcanoes are formed above the hot spot. In the Pacific Ocean, a hot spot has formed well away from plate boundaries and has created the volcanic Hawaiian Islands.

14 Volcanic activity is found in the following places:
- along ocean ridges where plates are moving apart, e.g. the mid-Atlantic ridge (volcanic activity on Iceland, for example)
- associated with rift valleys, e.g. the African rift valley (Mt Kilimanjaro and Mt Nyiragongo, for example)
- on or near subduction zones, e.g. the 'ring of fire' that surrounds the Pacific Ocean is associated with subduction
- over hot spots such as that in the middle of the Pacific Ocean which has given rise to the Hawaiian islands

15 Shield volcanoes have gentle sides and cover a large area. They are formed from basic lava that is free-flowing and thus can flow many kilometres from the fissure where emissions began. The Hawaiian Islands consist of shield volcanoes, the best known of which is Mauna Loa on Hawaii. In terms of volume and area, this is the largest volcano on the planet.

16 The following labels should be included:

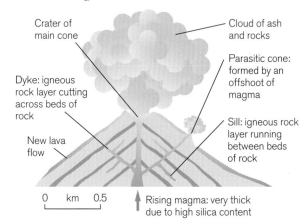

17 **Solfatara** are small volcanic areas where gases (mainly sulphurous) escape to the surface through vents and holes, e.g. around the Bay of Naples, Italy. Geysers occur when water, heated by volcanic activity, explodes onto the surface such as in the Yellowstone National Park, USA.

Hot springs and boiling mud — water, heated by volcanic action does not always explode onto the surface but comes up through springs. When this water mixes with fine surface deposits, boiling mud is formed.

18 The primary effects of a volcanic event are:
- lava flows
- tephra, which is solid material ejected into the atmosphere, varying in size from volcanic ash up to large volcanic bombs
- pyroclastic flows, which are extremely hot, gas-charged, high-velocity flows made from a mixture of gases and tephra
- volcanic gases, which include carbon dioxide, carbon monoxide, hydrogen sulphide, sulphur dioxide and chlorine

19 A **lahar** is a volcanic mudflow. This usually results from the melting of ice and snow during a major eruption and the mixing of this water with the deposits of the volcanic cone. These can rush downhill and devastate wide areas. Lahars formed during the eruption of Nevado del Ruiz in the Andes (Colombia) in 1985 killed over 20 000 people.

20 With some volcanoes there can be a build up of gases with magma pushing towards the surface but not reaching it. This build up can lead to a large explosion occurring which removes the summit of the volcanic cone, leaving a huge opening several kilometres across. This happened with Mt St Helens in 1980. When this happens to a volcanic island huge shock waves generate the sea waves known as tsunamis. These waves race across oceans, often devastating areas far removed from the original explosion. The large open area left behind is known as a caldera. The best example in modern times of such an event is that which devastated the island of Krakatoa in Indonesia (1883).

21 As the crust of the Earth is mobile, there tends to be a build up of stress within the rocks of which it consists. This pressure may be released suddenly, causing shock waves that result in an intense shaking of the surface. Conservative faults such as the San Andreas in California also experience earthquakes. Two plates are sliding past each other here and it is possible for this movement to 'stick'. When this is released and plate motion begins again, an earthquake is caused along the fault zone.

22 Seismic waves (P, S, and L) travel through the Earth from the epicentre of an earthquake and are recorded on a seismograph. The velocity of the waves depends on the density and elasticity of the medium through which they pass. The timing of the waves received at the seismograph has enabled scientists to locate the core of the Earth and determine other aspects of its interior (see diagram).

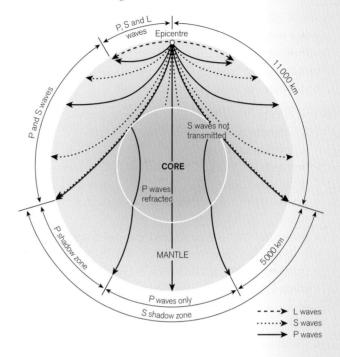

23 Earthquakes mainly occur:
- along plate boundaries, the most powerful being associated with margins where plates are converging
- along conservative margins which are represented on the surface by fault zones, the best known being the San Andreas fault in California (USA)
- along old fault lines such as the Malvern Lineament in the West Midlands of the UK

As plates move, tensions set up within them can be relieved by ground movements some distance from the boundaries. These are only minor earthquakes, e.g. Market Rasen (UK) in 2008.

Some seismologists think that human activity can trigger earthquakes — for example, building large reservoirs where the vast amounts of water put pressure on the surface rocks. The collapse of old deep-mine workings may also trigger an earthquake.

24 The **Richter scale** measures the magnitude of earthquakes. It is based on a logarithmic scale of 1 to 10. This means that an earthquake measuring 6 on the scale has a seismic wave amplitude ten times greater than that of an earthquake measuring 5 on the scale. In modern times, the Richter scale has been modified and in some cases other scales have been

adopted — for example, the United States Geological Survey (USGS) uses a movement magnitude scale for larger events; this scale gives similar results to the Richter.

25 When the ground is shaken violently, soil with a high water content loses its mechanical strength and starts to behave like a fluid. As a result of liquefaction, buildings that have their foundations in high water-content soils may collapse.

26 The effects of earthquakes on people and the built environment include the following:
- collapsing buildings
- destruction of roads, railways and other forms of communication
- destruction of service provision — electricity, gas, water
- fires resulting from fractured gas pipes and collapsed pylons
- flooding from dam breaches, levées etc.
- spread of disease, particularly from rotting corpses and pollution of water systems
- food shortages
- disruption to the local economy

Some of the above effects are short term; others can affect an area for a long time after the original event.

27 The impact of a tsunami is affected by:
- the distance the waves have travelled across the ocean and the length of the event which caused them
- the height of the wave when it hits the land
- the coastal physical geography, both offshore and on land
- coastal land use and population density
- the extent to which warnings can be given

28 One way to lessen the impact of a volcanic eruption is to try to protect against the effects. Another way is to try to predict when the eruption will occur so that areas can be evacuated and protection set in place. Some of the ways in which people can predict a volcanic eruption are:
- by studying the eruptive history of the volcano
- by studying the volcano closely, looking for certain gas emissions, groundwater levels and land swelling
- by measuring the shock waves which are generated by magma travelling towards the surface

29 People find it almost impossible to predict earthquakes (they can try to find an area that might have an earthquake, but at the moment it is not possible to say 'when'), so most management is directed towards protection from the event. This can be carried out in several ways:
- construct hazard-resistant structures, such as installing a large weight that can, with the aid of a computer programme, move to counteract stress on a building; build large rubber shock absorbers in the base of buildings; cross-brace buildings to strengthen when they shake
- retro-fit older buildings and elevated motorway sections with devices such as cross-bracing
- install smart meters to cut off gas supplies at a certain tremor threshold
- educate people in survival strategies and encourage earthquake drills in workplaces, schools etc.
- advise people how to assemble and store earthquake kits (to include such things as stored water, canned food, can/bottle opener, torch, matches, toilet paper, extra clothing and bedding, first-aid kit, batteries, small fire extinguisher)
- keep emergency services well prepared with specialised equipment (for searching rubble for people, heavy lifting gear etc.)
- land-use zoning, so that certain buildings (schools, hospitals etc.) are not constructed in the areas that are identified as being most at risk

30 Management measures for volcanic eruptions and earthquakes cost a great deal of money, which means that the inhabitants of wealthier countries are less vulnerable to such hazards. Volcanic and earthquake events, though, have a greater monetary cost to richer areas than to poorer ones, but in terms of the impact upon lives and an area's economy you would have to argue the opposite.

Example 1: In the 1989 Loma Prieta earthquake in California, in an area with earthquake-proof buildings, there were only a small number of deaths whereas in Armenia in 1988, an earthquake of similar size killed over 25 000 people, many of whom were crushed in buildings that had soft foundations and weak structures.

Example 2: In Kobe (Japan) in the earthquake of 1995 there was a large death toll from falling buildings, fires and disease. This was surprising because Japan was supposed to be in the forefront of earthquake management.

Other points include the following:
- In developing countries, poor people tend to be far more vulnerable than the richer people.

- The impact on poor people can last a long time as they struggle to rebuild their lives, often with very little help from the authorities.
- When such events happen, the poorer countries invariably need help from richer areas for medical supplies, specialist equipment and personnel trained to help in such circumstances.
- People in developed countries can reduce their own vulnerability and they can also take out insurance to cover losses, although this can be expensive for individuals.
- When these events occur, government aid and other forms of help are almost always available in developed countries. In California, for example, after an earthquake, help always comes from the state and from the national government in Washington.

Weather and climate and associated hazards

1 This question could be answered by using an annotated diagram. Whether answered by diagram or text, the following points should be made.
- **Troposphere:** lowest level and the one in which most weather processes operate
- Temperatures within the troposphere decrease with height. Its upper limit is known as the **tropopause** which is higher over the tropics than the poles (8 km to 17 km).
- **Stratosphere:** from the tropopause to around 50 km, its temperature increases with height to the top, which is known as the **stratopause**
- **Mesosphere:** temperature decreases again until the **mesopause** (80 km)
- Above the mesosphere is the **thermosphere** where temperatures again increase.

2 Low latitudes have a surplus of energy, but when you examine the higher latitudes (40° to the poles), you find that they have a net deficit, i.e. they lose more energy to space than they gain from it. They must obtain this heat from elsewhere. This situation is explained by the transfer of heat from low to higher latitudes through the medium of air (winds) and water (ocean currents). This is why the lower latitudes are not becoming hotter.

3 Hadley cells are the basis of tropical air circulation. There is one in each hemisphere and they have several components to their structure:

- Between the two Hadley cells there is the ITCZ where the air from each cell is forced upwards and is cooled. The water vapour condenses eventually, producing heavy rainfall.
- From the top of the ITCZ, the air moves polewards, circulating as an upper westerly wind around the planet as a result of the Coriolis effect.
- Around 30°N and 30°S this colder air begins to sink back to the surface. At the surface high pressure, known as the subtropical anticyclones, is created. The sinking air warms and any residual moisture is evaporated. The surface high pressure gives cloudless skies.
- Some of this descending air moves back towards the equator as the trade winds. These are also subject to the Coriolis effect, which gives them an easterly flow (northeast trades and southeast trades). This air then flows back into the ITCZ to complete the cycle of the Hadley cell (see diagram).

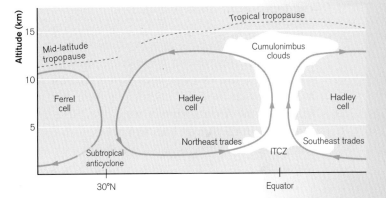

4 The oceanic circulation is part of the horizontal transfer of heat from the tropics to the polar regions (probably responsible for about 20% of the total transfer of heat within the energy budget). The main effects on climate are as follows:
- The movement of warm water across the northern oceans brings warmer winter conditions to the western sides of continents between latitudes 40° and 65°. This effect is seen particularly in the British Isles.
- The Labrador current brings a very cold effect down the eastern coast of Canada and on into the USA in winter.
- The cold currents of the southern oceans bring cooler conditions to the western coasts of southern Africa and South America. Onshore winds, after blowing over these currents, create foggy areas as water vapour is condensed through the cooling effect of the currents.

5 There are two major ways in which latitude affects climate:

- **length of daylight:** in the tropics, daylight stays around 12 hours per day throughout the year, whereas in polar areas there are long periods of continuous light or darkness. Between the equator and the poles, therefore, the length of night and day varies with latitude. As heat energy from the sun is only received during the day, the amount of daylight is an important factor in determining temperature.

- **angle of the sun:** the more vertical the sun's rays, the stronger they are. When they are vertical, these rays heat up a much smaller area than when they come in at an oblique angle. This gives more heat in the tropics than at the poles. It also explains why 6–8 hours of continuous winter sunshine on the British Isles does not have a great effect on temperatures.

6 The Gulf Stream/North Atlantic Drift brings warm water from the subtropics in a northeasterly direction towards the British Isles. Southwesterly winds blowing over this warmer water bring much milder conditions to the area in winter than is the case for most places on the same latitude (e.g. Labrador and Siberia). If the Arctic conveyor were disrupted, winter conditions in the British Isles would be much colder than at present. There is also a possibility with all this colder water, that summers could also be a little cooler. The British Isles would have a climate similar to that of northern Canada.

7 The weather associated with these air masses is as follows:

- **arctic:** very cold with snow in winter and early spring; often with very clear skies
- **polar maritime:** cold, moist weather; often unstable air associated with heavy showers
- **polar continental:** very cold temperatures in winter with snow in eastern England; warm conditions in summer
- **tropical maritime:** mild air in winter; often moist with stable conditions and low-lying cloud, possible advection fog on coasts
- **tropical continental:** hot, dry, heatwave conditions in summer

8 **Weather** is the day-to-day state of the atmosphere. It is the conditions (temperature, precipitation, cloud cover, wind speed and direction) occurring at a particular time, e.g. a cold showery morning with a strong westerly wind blowing. **Climate** is the average weather in an area, usually calculated by looking at data from a minimum of 30 years. It is the seasonal pattern of temperature and precipitation, e.g. the climate of the British Isles has mild winters with cool to warm summers.

9 a A **mid-latitude depression** is an area of low pressure that forms a system and is frequently experienced in the cool temperate western maritime climate (the climate of the British Isles). It contains rising air and precipitation associated with frontal systems. Winds blow anticlockwise within it (northern hemisphere).

b An **anticyclone** is a system of high pressure in which air sinks and diverges near the ground. Winds are generally light with a clockwise wind flow (northern hemisphere). Conditions are generally dry.

c A **front** is the dividing line between two different air masses.

10 a The winter was fairly mild with average temperatures not falling below 2°C (in January). Summer was cool with average temperatures not rising above 15°C. The year was generally wet with few months having less than 50 mm of rainfall.

There was no distinct dry season although the months of May, June and July had less rainfall than other 3-monthly periods. October was also quite dry (around 40 mm).

b Temperatures seem to be rather low for places in this climate. Large areas would have temperatures over 5°C in winter and close to 20°C in summer.

Rainfall was over 1400 mm, which is high. Parts of eastern England, for example, receive less than 600 mm and around 1000 mm falls in Cornwall. A cooler and wetter climate could be explained by the station's altitude being 380 m above sea level.

11 The weather associated with the passage of a depression can be broken down into four segments:

- **ahead of the warm front and its passage:** increasing and lowering cloud eventually brings light rain which becomes more continuous and heavy as the front approaches
- **warm sector:** noticeable warming after passage of the warm front with often overcast conditions and some light rain or drizzle
- **passage of the cold front:** large cumulonimbus clouds with a short period of heavy rainfall and possible hail and thunder

- **after the cold front:** temperatures drop noticeably with clouds breaking up into cumulus clouds that produce showers with clear intervals (see diagram)

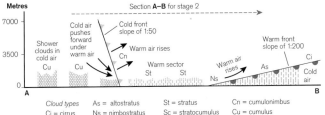

Cross-section through a depression

Cloud types As = altostratus St = stratus Cn = cumulonimbus
Ci = cirrus Ns = nimbostratus Sc = stratocumulus Cu = cumulus

12 a Station A has much less cloud than station B; it is raining at B; at B the temperature is cooler; at B the wind is stronger and southwesterly as opposed to north-westerly at A.

b Winter anticyclones result in:
- cold daytime temperatures (below freezing to a max of 5°C)
- very cold night-time temperatures (below freezing with frost)
- clear skies by both day and night
- radiation fog forming at night and possibly persisting all the following day
- generally calm conditions, often with pollutants trapped
- cold moist air may be trapped under the high pressure giving low-lying stratus cloud and contributing to 'anticyclonic gloom'

Summer anticyclones have the following features:
- warm to hot day-time temperatures (possibly over 25°C)
- warm night-time temperatures (may not fall below 15°C)
- clear skies with hazy sunshine in some areas
- early morning mists, fog and dew that vanish rapidly
- onshore winds in eastern England may cause sea frets (haars) in coastal regions

13 When you give information about the impact of a storm, it is important to give it within the following categories:
- impact on the physical landscape, i.e. storm damage on coastlines, trees blown down
- death toll
- structural damage to buildings
- impact upon transport and power supplies
- estimated cost to both the national and local economy (include insurance figures if available)

14 On such a question, you are required to *describe* the climate; you are *not* required to provide any reasons. If you include such material in your answer, the examiner will ignore it.

The general features of each climate are:
a equatorial: fairly high temperatures all year; hardly any seasonal variation; convectional rainfall often falling in the late afternoon; high rain totals (over 2000 mm); no real dry season
b tropical wet and dry: temperatures generally higher than equatorial; hot season is the wet time with heavy concentrated convectional rainfall; dry season is the cooler time
c tropical monsoon: high temperatures in the hot season; much lower temperatures in the cooler season; high rainfall totals in the wet season which usually corresponds with hotter times, although the highest temperatures are reached just before monsoon rains begin

Each description should be enhanced by the inclusion of detailed figures on temperature and precipitation.

15 The ITCZ is the point where the air movements known as the trade winds in the Hadley cells converge at the latitude of the equator. This converging air is unstable and rises, forming convective clouds that result in large downpours of precipitation. As the position of the overhead sun moves both north and south of the equator, the ITCZ follows this movement, taking its rainfall belt in the same direction. Therefore, its maximum northern extent occurs in June and its maximum southern extent in December. This explains why it is possible to have a tropical wet and dry climate as the ITCZ is responsible for the wet season.

16 Several conditions have to be present for such storms to develop:
- oceanic location with sea surface temperatures above 27°C — this provides the continuous source of heat to maintain rising currents of air
- ocean depth must be at least 70 metres — this provides enough moisture to give the latent heat to drive the system
- location at least 5° either side of the equator — this enables the Coriolis force to work at its maximum to bring about air rotation
- low-level convergence of air
- rapid outflow of air at higher levels pushing away the warm air that has risen through the storm

17 The distribution is seen on the following map:

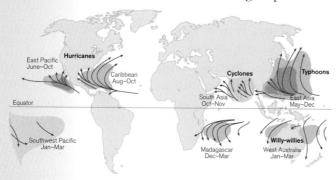

18 There are three main ways in which these storms pose a hazard:

- **High winds** can damage buildings, bridges, roads and transmission lines. Agricultural areas can be devastated and boats damaged. The winds hurl huge pieces of debris into the air which can kill people.
- **Heavy rainfall** causes severe flooding, landslides and mudslides.
- **Storm surges** flood low-lying coastal areas, particularly affecting large river deltas. Fishing fleets can be decimated and coastal buildings and port facilities wrecked. Flooding of coastal agricultural regions causes salt contamination which means that such areas take a long time to recover.

19 Dealing with the hazard involves prediction and protection, although there has been research into whether it is possible to seed hurricanes at sea to prevent them coming onshore with full force. **Prediction** lies with weather bureaus such as the national Hurricane Center in Florida, which collects data from satellites and from land- and sea-based recording stations. Weather surveillance aircraft are also important. This gives people warning and allows for evacuation. It is important to get it right because false alarms can cost millions of dollars. As for **protection**, in developing countries hurricane shelters can be provided and, in richer areas, sea walls and breakwaters can be strengthened. Land-use zoning is an attempt to prevent building in the most vulnerable areas.

20 An urban heat island is a warm spot in the 'sea' of surrounding cooler rural air. It is most noticeable at night, particularly when conditions are calm and clear in winter. It is created by:

- city surfaces, i.e. brick, stone and tarmac absorbing large quantities of heat by day. This is stored and released at night.
- heat coming from buildings, industries and vehicles. People also generate heat and there are many people in big cities. Heat generated by human activities and people is known as anthropogenic heat.
- pollution from buildings, vehicles and industry creating a 'dome' that retains heat

21 Description: temperature is highest in the city centre (over 3°C higher than rural surrounds); noticeable 'cliff' at edge of urban area where temperatures fall rapidly: surburban 'plateau' to left; plateau would have appeared to right but there is a noticeable dip where the park is situated

Explanations:

- city centre has highest temperatures because of density of buildings
- suburban plateau, as there tends to be a uniformity of building
- lower temperatures over park, as open area does not retain or put out heat
- steep drop to rural temperatures which are noticeably lower than those in the city (for the reasons given in the answer to Question 20).

22 Precipitation is higher over urban areas; convection rainfall tends to be heavier and more frequent in cities; higher incidence of thunder and lightning in urban areas; snow is less common in cities and it also melts faster.

23 Buildings exert a powerful frictional drag on air moving over and around them, which creates turbulence, giving rapid and abrupt changes in wind direction and speed; air is channelled into 'canyons' between high buildings (the Venturi effect); single buildings displace air upward and around the sides and air is also pushed downwards in the lee of the building; average wind speeds are lower than in the surrounding rural areas.

24 **Particulate pollution:** the solid matter in the atmosphere which is derived mainly from power stations and vehicle exhausts. Such particles are usually less than 25 um in diameter. Particulate pollution also includes cement dust, tobacco smoke, ash, coal dust and pollen. These very small pollutant particles are sometimes referred to as PM10s.

Photochemical smog: this is caused by the chemical reaction of sunlight on nitrogen oxides and hydrocarbons in exhaust gases which produces ozone

25 Some of the ways in which authorities have tried to control atmospheric pollution are:

- **vehicle control in inner urban areas:** traffic-free centres; park-and-ride schemes; congestion charges; driving restrictions, such as barring certain vehicles on certain days
- **more public transport:** mass-transit systems such as trams, bus-only lanes
- **clean air controls:** Clean Air Acts in the UK; Air Quality Management Areas; vegetation planting to capture particulates on leaves
- **zoning of industry**
- **vehicle emission legislation:** catalytic converters in cars; lead-free petrol

26 Sources that can produce evidence include:

- pollen analysis
- dendrochronology, i.e. analysis of tree rings
- ice-core analysis from areas of Greenland and Antarctica
- sea-floor analysis
- radiocarbon dating
- changing sea levels shown by rias, fjords and raised beaches
- glacial deposits
- historical records including paintings, parish records etc.

27 There are several theories that have attempted to explain climatic change.

Causes that have operated outside of the Earth have included variations in solar output (sunspot activity); changes in the Earth's orbit and axial tilt (this affects the amount of radiation reaching the surface); meteorite impact.

On the planet, it has been suggested that climatic change could be down to volcanic activity; plate movement; changes in oceanic circulation; changes in the gaseous composition of the atmosphere (such as increased carbon dioxide levels).

28 Global warming could affect the British Isles in the following ways:

- **more coastal flooding** (a result of higher sea levels and storm surges) would affect agriculture,

communications, coastal urban areas and power generation

- **agriculture:** some yields would decrease (possibly cereals), others would increase (possibly sugar beet, potatoes); growing season would increase giving higher productivity; new crops could be introduced; new pests would occur and there could be an increase in some pests present already
- **landscape:** different plant and animal species (with an increased number of foreign species); some native species may disappear being unable to adapt; species will migrate north and into higher altitudes; snow may become rare over the whole area (the Scottish mountains may have snow for only a few days every year)
- **soils:** higher temperatures could increase soil-moisture deficits; clay soils may shrink endangering the foundations of buildings; possibility of less organic matter in the soil
- **Water resources:** wetter winters could be beneficial but drier summers would have the opposite effect
- **Energy use:** warmer conditions would give rise to lower energy needs but there could be a growing demand for air conditioning

29 At a local scale, it is important that resources are used more wisely and that any development has sustainability as one of its major features. Local authorities can help to cut down carbon dioxide emissions by trying to reduce vehicle usage (the answer notes for Question 25, list several ways in which this can be done). At an individual level, people can contribute by insulating their homes to a higher standard; using energy wisely; recycling (which cuts down energy use); using their vehicles less frequently.

30 a A **carbon footprint** is the total amount of greenhouse gases produced in order to directly or indirectly support human activities. It is usually expressed in the equivalent tons of carbon dioxide. A personal carbon footprint is the sum of the emissions induced by a person's activity in a given time frame. This is related directly to the amount of natural resources consumed.

b This is to do with the level of development. Reference could be made to developed countries having high energy use coupled with widespread vehicle use. The USA and UK are almost the exact opposite of Tanzania. Energy provision in USA and

UK uses methods that release large amounts of carbon dioxide. China and India are also guilty of this, but in those countries the huge greenhouse gas emissions appear smaller because the figures are per capita and they have enormous populations. They are also much more developed than Tanzania, in that they are both industrialised (using large amounts of coal) and have greater vehicle use.

Ecosystems: change and challenge

1 An **ecosystem** is a community of plants and animals within a physical environment. An ecosystem can exist at any scale — for example from a single tree or a freshwater pond to a climax vegetation community. The various components of the ecosystem such as soils, vegetation, climate and animals are interrelated; energy flows occur in the system and materials such as nutrients are recycled and circulated between the soil, plants and leaf litter and as part of the food chain.

2 A **trophic level** is a link or stage of the energy transfer model known as a food chain. At each trophic level some energy is available as food for the next trophic level. Some of this energy is also lost in excreta, in the decay of dead organisms and in respiration.

3 Within all ecosystems, nutrients are required for plant growth and are recycled around the components in the system. Inputs include nutrients such as carbon and nitrogen in precipitation and minerals from weathered parent rock. Outputs include loss of nutrients from the system through the soil by leaching and by surface runoff. Flows or transfers of nutrients include leaf fall from the biomass to the litter, decomposition of litter, transfer of nutrients to the soil, and uptake of nutrients from the soil by trees and other plants.

4 There are four trophic levels within this food web and as the trophic levels increase in status, the number of consumers at each level generally declines. There are four consumer species at levels 1 and 2, and only two at levels 3 and 4. The food web is simple, with only one species having a varied diet (the Macleay's honeyeater). The quoll and the python are carnivores; most other species are herbivores.

5 **Succession** is a series of changes that take place in a plant community. In a primary succession,

the development begins on a surface that has not been vegetated previously. It is termed a secondary succession if the original vegetation has been cleared or destroyed naturally.

As the vegetation of an area develops and changes through time, the characteristics and species of plants alter until a balance is reached with the environmental conditions (soil and climate). This state is known as the **climatic climax** and does not change as long as the environmental conditions remain unchanged.

6 You are required to study one succession from the following: lithosere, psammosere, hydrosere and halosere. You should know the species involved in the succession and you should be able to explain how each stage changes over time. You should be aware of the processes involved in the transition. One way to learn this work more effectively is to use a diagram in which time increases from left to right, and the species named and processes identified, are above the timeline.

7 Tall trees are the dominant species. Oak is the tallest (and can reach 30–40 m) followed by elm, beech, sycamore, ash and chestnut. Trees develop large crowns and have broad but thin leaves. The trees are deciduous.

Most woodlands show some stratification. Below the canopy is a shrub layer with smaller trees such as holly, hazel, rowan and hawthorn. Just above the forest floor is a herb layer which is dense if the shrub layer allows enough light through. The herb layer is made up of grasses, bracken, ferns and some flowering plants, such as the bluebell, that appear early in the year before the trees have developed their full canopy. Epiphytes, such as lichens and mosses, grow on the trunks and branches of trees. On the forest floor mosses grow and a thick layer of leaf litter is readily broken down by the soil microbes and animals.

8 **Composition** of a vegetation type refers to the species that make it up. Where vegetation consists of only one species (e.g. a pine plantation) it is called a plant society. However, vegetation is usually made up of a number of species and is called a plant community. Tropical rainforests, where the conditions are warm and moist, contain several thousand plant species. **Structure** refers to the stratification or layering of a woodland (see also the answer to Question 7). For example, tropical rainforests have an emergent layer, a canopy layer and a ground layer.

9 Plant successions can be stopped from reaching the climatic climax, or deflected towards a different climax, by human interference. The resulting vegetation is known as a **plagioclimax**. Examples of human activities that create a plagioclimax include deforestation or afforestation, animal grazing or trampling, fire clearance. An example of a plagioclimax in the British Isles is heather moorland.

10 Salisbury Plain is an area where animal grazing has taken place for many years alongside its use by the military. Areas that have been left ungrazed have low diversity of plants and flies, as have areas that have only recently been grazed by sheep. As an area is grazed over longer periods of time then the species diversity of both plants and flies increases. Managing a plagioclimax, therefore, seems to increase richness of species and is good for biodiversity.

11 For example, Salisbury Plain is dry grassland developed on the shallow lime-rich soils of the chalklands that form the plain. The plain is not very fertile because of the lack of nitrogen and phosphorus and a wide variety of stress-tolerant species populate the most natural of the grasslands. It was bought for military training over 100 years ago and has not been subject to intensive farming, although the use for tank ranges and military exercises has affected plant communities. Today the herb-rich grasslands support 13 species of rare plants and 67 species of rare invertebrates. Towards the top of the food chain are birds such as quail, whinchat, stonechat, grasshopper warbler and skylark and rare birds including grey partridge, hobby and merlin and the great bustard, which was reintroduced in 2003.

12 You are required to study the biome of one tropical region (savanna grassland, tropical rainforest or tropical monsoon forest). When describing the characteristics of the vegetation you should refer to both composition and structure. For example, a brief summary of the vegetation of the savanna would be:
- Trees dominate over grasses where the wet season is longer.
- Grasses (e.g. elephant grass) dominate in locations where the dry season is longer. Grasses may be over 2 m tall, with long roots reaching down to underground moisture.
- Both grasses and trees are deciduous, losing their leaves in the dry season.
- Trees have adapted to survive drought — for example, baobabs store water in their swollen

trunks to survive the dry season.
- Trees develop xerophilous features: deep, branched roots seek moisture underground.
- Evergreen trees also occur, with hard leathery leaves that reduce transpiration loss.
- Acacia trees have developed flattened crowns, which cope with the strong trade winds.
- Vegetation has adapted to cope with fire.

13 Make sure you draw an annotated diagram to support your answer. The diagram should show the relationship between precipitation and potential evapotranspiration (as two line graphs) over a period of a year. Depending on the chosen biome, some or all of the following terms should be used: soil moisture deficit, soil moisture recharge, soil moisture utilisation and soil moisture surplus. Make reference to the impact of each of these on other aspects of hydrology (such as river discharge) within the area concerned, and also to how plants and animals adapt to the changes.

14 The key here is to make sure that you link plants to the climate. For example, for the tropical rainforest biome:

The trees such as teak and mahogany grow rapidly upwards towards the light and their trunks are slender with few branches. The bark is thin because the trees do not need protection from cold winter temperatures. The tallest trees have flexible trunks that allow a good deal of movement. This is necessary because at 50 m above ground level the winds can be quite strong and flexible trunks allow the trees to sway without breaking. Since the minerals that the trees need are found only in the top layer of the soil and there is an abundant supply of water from rainfall, the tree roots do not penetrate the soil to any great depth. They tend to spread out on the forest floor. Buttress roots, that emerge up to 3 m above the ground, help to stabilise the tallest trees. The leaves have adapted to the climate, in particular to the regular heavy rainfall, by developing drip-tips. These allow excess water to be shed easily. In addition, some leaves are thick and leathery to withstand the strong sunlight and prevent too much loss of water from the plant.

15 The amount of rainforest lost in the countries varies greatly. Most losses are in South America, and least in Africa, from a small amount (17 000 ha) in the Congo to a large amount in Brazil (2 309 000 ha). (Percentage changes could be used here.) Although Brazil has lost

the greatest area of rainforest, as a proportion of the total, in comparison with the other countries shown, this is a relatively low percentage. All the countries shown have forest in over half their area, even after the losses. Malaysia and Cameroon have the largest percentage losses, with the latter seemingly most at risk because of its lower base. It is also worth noting that despite the media hype of the extent of deforestation in tropical areas, the actual extent is low.

16 **Biodiversity** is the range of wild and cultivated species within an ecosystem. Such diversity has recently become a major environmental issue because environments are being degraded at an accelerating rate and biodiversity is being reduced through the destruction of natural habitats.

For example, within the tropical monsoon forests biodiversity is as follows:

- The most continuous untouched monsoon forest remains in Myanmar, Thailand, Laos, Vietnam and Cambodia; more than 90% has been deforested in India.
- Common species of trees and other plants include teak, sal, bamboo and orchid.
- There are fewer species of mammals, birds, reptiles, fish and amphibians than in tropical rainforest and savanna grasslands. Species include Bengal tiger, Indian elephant, leopard, rhinoceros, python and cobra, all of which are subject to losses from hunting and destruction of habitat.

17 Make sure that you link the impact of development on your chosen biome with the concept of sustainability — namely the degree to which the environment can be protected and/or managed for the future. The loss of tropical rainforest has extensive impacts:

- As habitats shrink, plant species become endangered.
- Some animal species, for example tigers and orang-utans, are threatened by extinction.
- The vegetation protects the latosol soils from the regular heavy tropical downpours. Once the trees are removed, the topsoil is open to erosion and to leaching of nutrients and minerals.
- The microclimate of the forest is disturbed by deforestation. The daily water cycle of rapid evapotranspiration followed by afternoon precipitation cannot occur and there is less cloud cover, so the temperature range becomes greater.

- Burning associated with forest clearance leads to local air pollution, including smogs.

Indonesia and Malaysia have industrialised rapidly and economic development is occurring quickly. Clearance of forest has made space for new industrial developments. Income from the export of hardwood logged from the forest has resulted in greater prosperity for many. In Brazil, raw materials mined in the rainforest have provided valuable export earnings to help pay off debt, but more forest has disappeared as a result.

Indigenous people have seen their traditional way of life changed as deforestation has destroyed their culture and in some cases forced them to move from their land. In the Amazon basin, many Amerindians, such as the Kayapo, have been forced into reservations. Some have left the rainforest to try their luck in the big cities of the southeast. As they have come into contact with the outside world disease has ravaged some indigenous populations. Lack of immunity to Western diseases, for example measles, has meant the loss of entire villages.

18 An **urban niche** is an area that provides an individual habitat for specific plants and animals unique to that urban area. For example, areas of bare tarmac, brick walls, barren wasteland and sides of transport routes (roadsides and alongside railway tracks) are urban niches.

19 Urban growth has provided a variety of new habitats on which ecosystems can develop. They include:
- industrial sites
- derelict sites
- residential gardens and allotments
- parks, transport routes (canals, roadside verges and railway lines)
- urban forests
- bodies of water, such as lakes and reservoirs

You should choose any two of these (or any other) and describe how the ecosystem (plants, animals etc.) that has evolved is different from the natural ecosystem. Do not forget the importance of fauna in an ecosystem. Suburban gardens are oases for songbirds, small mammals (e.g. hedgehogs, voles and bats) and amphibians (frogs, newts and toads). Even brownfield sites prove remarkably attractive to wildlife. Weeds provide food for insects and seed-eating birds, and on disturbed sites, lack of competition may allow more exotic species such as orchids to flourish.

20 In some ways, the processes are not different. The initial stages involve colonisation by mosses and lichens, as in a lithosere. However, windblown seeds from plants already in the urban environment, such as Oxford ragwort, buddleia and dandelion, can take root. As these plants die off, they produce a thicker and more nutrient-rich soil. Plants such as rosebay willowherb take hold. The processes are therefore similar — it is the species that are different. Alien plants such as Japanese knotweed invade the area in thickets, shading out most species beneath them. Finally, scrub woodland develops with willow in the more moist areas and birch in the drier. Brambles develop in large thickets — they grow rapidly and can access crevices in concrete.

21 In the specification, roads and railways are given as examples, but you could refer to other routeways if you wish. Motorways are often stated to have developed their own ecologies. The roadsides may be grassed and some species may become tolerant of the high salt content following gritting. Voles, mice and rabbits have colonised many motorway verges. At junctions, some areas are vegetated by planted bushes, shrubs and small trees, with cotoneasters and *Berberis* often being used because they are slow growing and easy to manage. These attract berry-eating birds. Kestrels are common sights above motorway verges because they feed on the small creatures mentioned above.

22 Public gardens, parks and cemeteries are all areas where the vegetation is managed. New plant species have been introduced, many from overseas such as the rhododendron and roses. In addition, many such areas — for example, Roundhay Park in Leeds — have flower gardens, herb gardens, walled gardens (with imported species of fruit) and scented gardens, the intention being to make the site attractive to visitors. Some authorities have also established arboretums. You should provide some detail of one area you have studied that has several species introduced from overseas.

23 Cities are centres for the establishment and spread of foreign species. One survey of a small urban common in Sheffield recorded the following species:
- from North America — Canadian goldenrod, Michaelmas daisy
- from Europe — sycamore, laburnum, wormwood, goat's-rue
- from China and Japan — buddleia, Japanese knotweed

Such species could have been introduced to the area by escapes from gardens, plants brought in by collectors or gardeners, windblown seed, or seed carried by animals and forms of transport. You should provide similar information for an area you have studied.

24 Make sure you refer to an area of rural–urban fringe that you have studied. A suitable example would be Birchwood, which is an area to the east of Warrington that was developed in the 1980s as a business park. Here, the green infrastructure of the area was planned and put in place before the start of the development. The vegetation has now matured and has produced an attractive area within which industrial complexes have been built. Housing areas nearby are shielded by the vegetation and many of the individual complexes are shielded from each other. Even areas of car parking are hidden from view from the roads serving the estate and in some cases from each other. There is also a planned walkway system through the middle of the business park that allows workers and others to enjoy a pleasant setting in the midst of an industrial area on the rural–urban fringe.

25 You are required to study one ecological conservation area in detail. Make sure that you know what aspects of the environment are being conserved and how the managers are attempting to do this. In many cases, managers encourage tourist and educational visits to the conservation area. You should be aware of how these activities are arranged. You should be able to comment on the success or otherwise of the area, making reference to each separate aspect of the scheme.

26 There are several global threats to biodiversity (with examples) including:
- habitat destruction — forest clearances, urban growth, mining of coral reefs
- climate change — melting of the ice sheets and warming of the permafrost
- diseases of plants and animals — transmission between wild and domesticated animals
- overexploitation — overfishing, illegal wildlife trade, rainforest logging
- introduction of alien species in areas where there is no natural predator
- pollution — overloading of agricultural nutrients affecting rivers and lakes

27 In the context of vegetation:
- a fragile environment is one that lacks resilience to change
- conservation refers to the protection and possible enhancement of the natural environment
- exploitation refers to the utilisation of an environment for commercial gain, which may involve its destruction or modification

28 Komodo's zoning plan creates areas with no human activity (core areas) and areas with intensive activity such as tourism, diving, settlement, fishing and traditional use of land, such as farming. Between these extremes lies a wilderness buffer zone, both terrestrial and marine. Zonation such as this is designed to create untouched wildlife reserves while also allowing tourists to visit and local people to continue to earn a living. These policies may lead to conflict. The management of the Komodo National Park raises interesting questions. Should the park be self-funding? Should an entrance fee be introduced? The fees could be used to construct visitor facilities and improve the visitor experience. Should an aim be to focus on expanding ecotourism? Some of the entrance fee finance could be invested in wells, schools, a mobile doctor and other facilities that would be welcome additions in this isolated and poor area.

29 You are required to study two case studies of contrasting fragile environments in terms of their management. For each case study, you should:
- know the characteristic features of the environments being managed
- know the strategies by which they are being managed
- be able to provide some statement of how successful they have been *vis-à-vis* their stated aims

The task of this question is then to compare these strategies in terms of their success. Most strategies will have a range of aims — for example, to conserve wildlife, to provide tourist opportunities or to raise incomes for locals. Each area will have varying degrees of success for each aim, and it is the degrees of success that you should compare.

30 This question asks you to consider the balance between conservation and exploitation in one case study of a fragile environment. An example could be the Gazi Women Mangrove Boardwalk project on the Kenyan coast. The challenge here is to balance the need for conservation and the need for economic growth. Industries which damage the mangrove forests, such as salt mining, also boost the local economy. One solution is to have community-based associations that replant mangrove seedlings and which also run other facilities such as a nursery school, and an ecotourism venture to help sustain local people. Research it at **www.mangroveactionproject.org**.

World cities

1 A millionaire city is one that has more than 1 million people. In 2009, there were 487 such cities in the world, 107 of which were in China (61) and India (46). Therefore, Asia has by far the largest number of millionaire cities. The continents of North America (59) and Europe (63) having similar numbers.

2 A mega city is a city with over 10 million people. There were 28 in 2009. Most of these (18) were in the developing world. Istanbul and Shanghai are examples. A world city is one that is connected commercially and technologically with similar cities in the world. Together they are globally powerful and have a huge influence in terms of trade, political strength and innovation. Examples include London, New York and Tokyo.

3 A starting point might be to highlight developed world cities (i.e. Tokyo, New York, Los Angeles, Osaka, Moscow). Note that these cities have populations that are either growing only slowly or are projected to be stable by 2015. Cities in developing Asia (e.g. Mumbai, Delhi, Shanghai, Kolkata, Dhaka) are projected to grow rapidly. There are only two African cities in the list — Cairo and Lagos. Lagos has the most rapid growth of any city listed.

4 It is true that as Asian, South American and African countries have become more developed the percentage of the population living in cities has increased. Urbanisation is increasing most rapidly in Africa and Asia. However, developed areas of the world that have already urbanised (Europe and North America) have falling rates of urbanisation as the trend towards living away from cities has become more popular. Hence the relationship is not clear cut.

5 **Urbanisation** is the increase in the proportion of a country's population that lives in towns and cities.

Suburbanisation is the movement of people from living in the inner parts of a city to living on the outer edges, or in areas between radial routes from the centre.

Counterurbanisation is the movement of people from large urban areas into smaller urban areas or into rural areas, leapfrogging the rural–urban fringe.

6 Reasons for the growth of a city may include natural factors (birth rates, mortality rates) and migration factors (push–pull). You would be awarded credit for both these types of factor. The key aspect here is that higher marks will be reserved for reasons that are specific to the city named. Make sure that you know some facts that have contributed to the growth of your chosen city — for example, types (or names) of industries that have attracted migrants.

7 Using Cairo as an example, the main effects of rapid urbanisation are:
- 30% of the city has no public sewage system; 55% of waste water is untreated and travels through open canals and rivers to the sea.
- Although the city does not have extensive areas of squatter settlements (examples include Bulaq and Chobra), many people live in inappropriate locations — for example, in the Cities of the Dead (the tombs of old Cairo) and on rooftops in makeshift dwellings.
- There is serious air pollution, caused by dense traffic and open-air cooking stoves.
- Waste disposal is disorganised. In some areas, it is carried out by the zabbaleen (waste collectors) using donkey carts.

8 Management solutions to these effects in Cairo include:
- a project to repair existing sewers and to extend the system to those parts of the city not served currently
- the provision of pipes carrying clean water into the Cities of the Dead and to the rooftop homes
- the provision of low-cost accommodation in high-rise flats in new satellite towns in the desert such as 'Ramadan 10' and '15 May'
- schemes to reduce the numbers of vehicles on the road, in particular by extending the underground metro system
- the organisation of a subsidised waste collection and recycling system across the city, giving the zabbaleen funds to purchase additional carts

9 There are significant variations within this city in the developing world:

- Chickpet is a typically Indian area of the city — bustling, high-density, established population, with all the problems of an old cramped city
- Basavanagudi is where the higher castes live — the wealthy, educated families. This may have also been the old colonial quarter.
- Bagular and Yelankha are densely populated shanty towns (bustees). The former is well established; the latter is new. There is a high percentage of migrants, low literacy levels and poor services. Overall, the quality of life is very low.
- Indiranagar is the area where the young, well-educated, highly paid workers in the computer-based industries, at the technology park, live. It seems 'Westernised'.

10 Make sure that you write about an actual place you have studied. Impacts could include:
- the development of housing estates (private and council) around a transport route (rail, bus, road)
- the provision of services, such as shops, schools and parks
- the growth of small industrial areas or warehousing
- the increased level of traffic congestion in the area

11 **Counterurbanisation** is a more recent phenomenon in small towns and villages. The impacts of this process include:
- an increase in use of a commuter railway station in the area, including the provision of car parking
- a rapid rise in the value of property in the area
- the construction of executive housing and, in some cases, gated housing
- the conversion of former farm and small industrial buildings (such as mills) into exclusive residences
- an increase in the number and range of exclusive shops and services

12 The role of technology in the process of counterurbanisation includes:
- effective rail links between small towns and city centre
- the electrification of railways
- the development of fuel-efficient vehicles
- the internet allowing home-working
- teleworking, as high-speed broadband becomes more available

13 **Re-urbanisation** is the process whereby the population decline in some areas of large towns and cities is being slowed down, or even reversed so that the population begins to grow again. It represents a movement of population towards the central-city area

with a rise in the number of housing developments. In the UK, it is associated with redevelopment and regeneration, often in the form of city-centre apartments and waterside developments, and increased employment in the financial and service sectors.

14 You must refer to a city that you have studied in detail. You should be able to give precise detail of the range of regeneration strategies that have been adopted in that city and provide clear evaluative statements of their success, or otherwise. Higher-level responses will discuss variations in the success over time, or space, or both.

15 The developers have regenerated Cardiff's city centre's historic Brains Brewery, closed in 2000, into the 'Old Brewery Quarter'. The photo shows a typical mix of bars, restaurants and apartments incorporating the regenerated brewery building, dating from 1887. Notice the prevalence of expensive stainless steel, glass and natural stone paving. Cardiff, like many UK cities, has focused on high-end housing, leisure, tourism and retail spending as the key to reinventing its city centre as a vibrant urban space, fit for the twenty-first century.

16 Any four of the following would qualify:
- high population out-migration figures
- many empty, boarded-up or derelict shops and properties
- the closing of schools, particularly primary schools, and low levels of educational attainment and aspiration
- high unemployment
- high incidence of crime, vandalism and graffiti
- low levels of participation in local democracy

17 Economic decline includes:
- movement of employment away from the large conurbations to smaller urban areas and to rural areas, and overseas
- the growth of service industries in rural areas and small towns

Population loss and social decline includes:
- out-migration of younger, aspirant people from inner-city areas
- a poor physical environment
- areas of low-quality housing, empty and derelict properties, vacant factories and unsightly, overgrown wasteland; high levels of vandalism and dereliction

All these factors contribute to a bleak landscape that is unattractive to investors.

18 **Gentrification** is a process of housing improvement. It is associated with a change in neighbourhood composition in which low-income groups are displaced by more affluent people, usually in professional or managerial occupations. It can be identified by the refurbishment of old houses and streets, a change in the nature of some services (e.g. pubs and shops to bars and restaurants), and an increase in the number of 'designer' outlets for both fashion and internal fixtures and fittings.

19 Property-led regeneration involved autonomous urban development corporations (UDCs) which were given responsibility for infrastructure renewal and derelict-site remediation in order to attract private sector investment. UDCs were free from many planning regulations and local and national government involvement was minimal.

Partnerships such as Regional Development Agencies work to combine private and public investment to regenerate key sites. Flagship and landmark buildings are used to 'kick-start' interest in an area. Many partnerships aim to create sustainable communities.

20 Reasons for the establishment of out-of-town retailing areas include:
- increased access to the wealthier suburban population
- cheaper land for site and expansion
- access to new roads/motorways
- advantage of derelict land grants (brownfield sites)
- high levels of dereliction in inner-city areas/CBDs
- difficulty of access to CBDs for shoppers and deliveries
- possibility of developing new attractive greenfield sites

21 In many small towns the impact of the decentralisation of retailing has been great. There has been a general decline, with the closure of small independent, often family-owned, shops. In particular, food retailers, electrical stores and small DIY shops have suffered. Boarded-up shops have increased in numbers, as have charity shops. However, despite negative predictions, in large towns the impact has been less. The CBDs of such towns and cities appear to have responded positively and 'fought back'. Many are now as vibrant as before, often showing the signs of extensive redevelopment.

You could illustrate your answer with reference to examples.

22 A range of issues has arisen:
- the redevelopment and/or clearance of farmland or a brownfield site
- the creation of extensive car parks and the roads leading to them
- the construction of a link to a motorway interchange and/or other transport interchange facilities
- further expansion of linked activities (e.g. cinemas)
- opportunities for employment for people living nearby
- increase in traffic and pollution, including noise of deliveries through the night
- issues of safety

You could illustrate any of these points with references to examples.

23 It is important to give precise information about the out-of-town retailing area you have studied. Include some or all of the following: the name(s) of the motorway and details of other transport links; the size of area covered; the nature of the area covered; the peculiarities of that particular centre (e.g. the central Oasis at Meadowhall); detail of any issues or problems that have arisen since its construction (e.g. traffic congestion on the M60 for the Trafford Centre).

24 A number of strategies are being devised to help reverse the decline of city centres, including:
- the establishment of business and marketing management teams
- the provision of a more attractive shopping environment with pedestrianisation, new street furniture, floral displays and landscaping
- the construction of all-weather shopping malls, attractive open street markets, cultural quarters and arcades
- the extensive use of CCTV and emergency alarm systems to reduce crime
- the organisation of shopping events such as Christmas fairs, late-night and Sunday shopping — sometimes referred to as 'the 24-hour city'

25 It is important to give precise information about the town-centre retailing area you have studied. Include some or all of the following: the means of access and details of other transport links; the size of the area covered; the nature of the area covered; the peculiarities of that particular centre — for example,

the use of certain flagship stores (e.g. Harvey Nichols in Leeds and Bristol) or other centrepieces; details of any issues or problems that have arisen since its construction (e.g. effects on other parts of the central area that are now seemingly 'ignored').

26 There are a number of ways in which urban areas can manage their waste: try to reduce it; reuse materials; recycle materials; burn some of it to create heat for housing and offices; compost it; bury it in the ground (landfill); or export it. You should try to elaborate on each of the three ways you choose.

27 Issues raised include:
- a rapid increase in the amount of waste being produced, possibly due to the rising consumerism of the people
- a huge proportion being placed in landfill — effects on the environment, smells, sights and water supplies
- 10% incinerated — this would be a large amount and have effects on air quality
- a relatively low amount being reprocessed into fertiliser (bio-treated); this could be increased, but at what cost?

28 The assumption here is that you have studied the waste management of one urban area, possibly the area where you live. All urban areas in the UK have to meet EU targets for recycling. You should be able to provide detail of how this urban area manages its waste — for example, where the landfill sites are, the number and location of household waste disposal sites, even the ways in which recyclable materials are sorted. You should then make a statement that summarises your response to the question.

29 Car ownership has increased significantly in recent years. Problems caused include:
- a high proportion of the population work in urban areas but live in rural or suburban areas, which causes problems associated with commuter traffic
- many journeys to work are around and across cities — public transport may not be developed for this
- economic growth has led to more commercial vehicles on the roads
- people often use their vehicles to access leisure and education facilities (e.g. the 'school run')
- atmospheric pollution which can lead to bronchial complaints and eye irritation. Asthma is an increasing problem around the world, possibly exacerbated by traffic fumes. Concentrations of low-level ozone

are increasing which can lead to photochemical smog (e.g. Los Angeles).

30 A wide range of transport management systems exist that could be studied: new road schemes (e.g. the M25), restricted access schemes (e.g. the congestion charge); traffic management schemes (e.g. park and ride, bus lanes); mass transit systems (e.g. the Metrolink). Make sure that you give precise details of your chosen system and offer a statement of its success, or otherwise.

Development and globalisation

1 a **GDP** stands for gross domestic product and is a commonly used measurement of development in a country. It represents the total value of all finished goods and services produced by a country in a year, usually expressed in amount per head of population.

b 'Third world' is a term, usually used in the past, which refers to all the poorer countries of the world. It is now usually replaced by **developing world**, although many see this term as too simplistic within the development continuum.

c **NICs** are newly industrialised countries. They have gone through this process within the last 40–50 years. Some books refer to 'industrialising' instead of 'industrialised' to imply that the process is still continuing.

2 The more developed countries have higher levels of economic growth and GNP, but lower levels of population growth and infant mortality. Poorer countries have the opposite of this and therefore a **development gap** has grown between these two groups of countries. This gap has increased with time.

3 As countries develop, they pass from one stage to another. The transition tends to be gradual with no sudden improvements in living standards. Therefore, there is a process, with countries at various stages of development and developing in different ways. This whole state is now often referred to as the **development continuum**.

4 **Globalisation** is the increasing interconnectedness in the world's economic, cultural and political systems. One commentator described it as the way in which people's lives are increasingly intertwined in economic, political and cultural terms with distant people and places.

5 In the early 1950s, over 90% of the world's manufacturing was concentrated in the developed economies. As large companies grew in those areas, they began to search the world for cheaper manufacturing locations. TNCs developed, making foreign direct investment (FDI) in many countries of the then developing world. This move has been referred to as global shift. Transfer of technology has enabled such countries to increase their productivity, making them even more attractive to foreign investment. Now, in the early twenty-first century, over 50% of all manufacturing employment is in the developing world.

6 **Global marketing** is marketing on a world-wide scale. Companies involved view the world as one market, creating products that fit the various regional marketplaces. The ultimate goal is to sell the same product everywhere. A good example is the drinks manufacturer Coca-Cola.

7 The advantages of the Asian Tigers were:
- well-developed infrastructure such as roads, railways and harbour facilities
- relatively well-educated people who possessed skills
- government support, offering cheap loans etc.
- good geographical locations
- cultural traditions that admire education and achievement
- less rigid laws and regulations on labour, taxation and pollution which allowed more profitable operations for TNCs

8 In countries in the initial phase of NIC development, wage levels began to rise, increasing the operating costs for TNCs. New countries were sought, where wage levels were low but where recent improvements in infrastructure had taken place. In the Asian Tigers, home companies had grown to the point where they too were looking to reduce their operating costs and move overseas. In South Korea, a number of large companies known as chaebols (e.g. Samsung) had developed along these lines.

9 Reasons that TNCs looked towards China to invest include:
- government encouragement, as it moved the country from a centrally planned economy to a more market-orientated system
- the extremely large labour force
- special economic zones (SEZ) were established

where foreign companies could get preferable tax rates

- China joined the WTO in 2001, giving greater access to global markets with a resulting trade boom

10 India's economic growth has been based more on the service sector than on manufacturing. At the beginning of the twenty-first century, around 50% of India's GDP was accounted for by the service sector. FDI in India occurred mainly in the software and IT services sector. India leads the world in 'back-office' functions — the IT-enabled services (call centres, accounts offices, data entry and conversion, and knowledge services).

11 In the early twenty-first century there is a new evolving stage in which new markets are emerging. Countries such as Brazil, United Arab Emirates (UAE), Chile, Saudi Arabia and Russia are good examples of such changes. The momentum for these changes has been the need to raise living standards, give increased opportunities to the local population and to attract foreign investment into countries. Several of these countries are moving from centralised political and economic systems to more open-market situations.

12 The following points could be made:
- poverty has fallen considerably (judged by this criterion)
- very high figures in 1973–74 with over half the population of India receiving less than $1 per day
- urban poor always at a lower percentage than the poor in rural areas
- both areas show a similar pattern of decline, although the gap between urban and rural has decreased over this period
- in 1973–74 the difference was large (urban 49% and rural 56.4%)
- in 1999–2000 the difference was much smaller (urban 23.6% and rural 27.1%)
- overall figures still large by 2000 in the light of India's huge population (over 1 billion by 2000)

13 LDCs are defined by the following:
- low incomes, measured at below $800 GDP per capita (3-year average)
- human resource weaknesses in the fields of nutrition, health, education and literacy: low-life expectancy, low calorie per capita intake, low

school enrolment particularly at the secondary level and low levels of adult literacy
- economic vulnerability shown by little economic diversification; this is based on the numbers of people involved in manufacturing, share of manufacturing in the GDP, levels of energy consumption and merchandise export concentration levels (high levels of raw materials)

14 The quality of life is so low because most people live in such poverty. These people have an income that is too small to meet their basic needs. In 2005, it was estimated that 277 million people within the LDCs were living on less than $1 per day. Resources are low and, even if they could be equally divided, they are insufficient to provide the needs of the population on a sustainable basis. The economic freedom of the majority of the population is, therefore, seriously constrained. Some people aspire to, and reach for, better things, but the high population growth rate means that the number of people living in extreme poverty continues to increase.

15 Some of these countries suffer from ongoing and widespread conflict, which includes civil wars and ethnic conflict. The violence in the Darfur area of Sudan is a good example. Governments are often corrupt and aid money does not reach the people for whom it was intended. The governments of many of these countries are authoritarian with dictatorships in place. This means that it is often impossible to resolve issues, resulting in a great deal of political and social instability. Many are landlocked, e.g. Niger.

16 By borrowing money from the 1970s onwards, many LDCs ran up enormous debts. With high-interest payments further increasing the debts, there was little hope of repayment. By 1996, the IMF and others had produced the Heavily Indebted Poor Countries programme (HPIC) which provided some breathing space and low-interest loans to reduce such debts to sustainable levels. The G8 countries also proposed to cancel the debts of HIPCs in a scheme known as Multilateral Debt Relief Initiative (MDRI). To qualify for such a scheme eligible countries had to meet stiff criteria — poverty reduction programmes, public expenditure management systems and better use of public resources had to be in place.

17 Countries seek to further their economic development by looking for alliances that would stimulate trade between countries and provide other economic

benefits. This should lead eventually to improved living standards. This is how trade blocs were set up. In some cases, these have led to greater economic and social cooperation between countries across a range of areas such as agriculture, transport, industry, energy resources, pollution and regional development.

18 The EU began life in 1957 as the European Economic Community (EEC — the 'Common Market') on the signing of the Treaty of Rome. The original six members were France, Italy, West Germany, Belgium, the Netherlands and Luxembourg. Its physical expansion occurred at irregular intervals. The UK, Ireland and Denmark joined in 1973 with Greece following in 1981. The EEC expanded to the southwest in 1986 taking in Spain and Portugal. The EU was established in 1993 and expanded northwards and eastwards in 1995 when Finland, Sweden and Austria joined. The biggest expansion came in 2004 when ten countries joined, these being Cyprus, Czech Republic, Estonia, Hungary, Latvia, Lithuania, Malta, Poland, Slovakia and Slovenia. This represented a major expansion into the east of Europe. The latest expansion came in 2007 when Bulgaria and Romania became members.

19 The negative consequences of the grouping of nations include:
- decisions can be centralised, leading to a loss of sovereignty for individual nations
- some loss of financial controls to a central authority, such as a central bank
- legislation handed down from the centre with pressure for individual countries to accept what they feel might be against their national interest
- some resources (e.g. fish) have to be shared, which may lead to economic sectors in certain countries suffering
- elites within the system can hold a disproportionate amount of power through the voting system
- some countries might want to drive towards federalism, while other countries are vehemently opposed
- smaller and remote regions may feel left out by central organisations, which may lead to greater voices for separatism

20 TNCs are companies that operate in more than one country. Headquarters of these companies are usually found in the country of origin, while manufacturing plants are found in other countries. Research and development (R&D) is also found in the home country, but as an organisation becomes bigger and more widespread, R&D centres can also develop in other regions.

21 The following points could be made:
- The original manufacturing plants would have been in Japan.
- Some of the countries shown — for example, Indonesia, Kenya, Thailand and Malaysia — are cheaper labour locations.
- There are manufacturing plants in the large North American and European markets (UK and Spain). In the case of the UK and Spain, Nissan is considered to be a European manufacturer because it builds the vehicles within the EU. It therefore avoids import restrictions.
- There will be markets in developing countries such as South Africa and Egypt which plants in those countries will supply.
- There are emerging markets where incomes are rising and therefore there is an increasing market for vehicles. Nissan plants will supply those local markets in Brazil, Russia, India and China.

22 India is attractive to FDI because there are liberal investment policies in place and the country is seen as being innovative and increasingly producing technologically advanced products. It is also a low-cost destination. The service sector has been important in India's economic growth, and this report shows that FDI in services has contributed enormously to that growth.

23 In many countries, the largest share of inward investment through FDI is now accounted for by the service sector. The continued process of deregulation and liberalisation has allowed FDI into areas that were once dominated by state or domestic private-sector firms. Therefore, a growing number of the world's largest TNCs are to be found in the service sector, particularly banks, insurance and retailing organisations. The ICT revolution has also opened up overseas investment in tradeable services. IT-enabled services, for example, are now increasingly globalised because information can be sent easily around the world and service components can be located in the most efficient and cost-effective places.

24 Impacts can be both positive and negative. Positive impacts include:
- employment

- multiplier effects, where local investment can trigger more employment through the process known as cumulative causation
- more disposable income in a region (because of wages etc.) which can generate more demand, producing an upward spiral in economic terms
- new methods of working can be introduced
- transfer of technology to the host country, creating a more skilled workforce

Negative impacts include:

- possible destruction of local firms and with this, many jobs
- damage to the environment where pollution laws are less strict
- exploitation of labour by, in some cases, paying low wages to a non-unionised workforce
- removal of capital, generated by the TNC, back to the home country
- decisions made in the interests of the TNC that are not always favourable to the host country
- increased urbanisation as the rural poor flock to urban areas seeking employment provided by TNCs

25 As with the answer to Question 24, impacts can be both positive and negative. In this case, the negative side usually dominates. This is because there could be a large loss of employment as the TNC closes factories in its home country. This leads to less disposable income in certain regions resulting in an economic downward spiral (vicious circle), with the multiplier effect working in reverse. This can also happen to service employment, such as call-centre operations.

On the positive side, high-salaried posts in administration and R&D are created at headquarters. Profitable companies return their profits to the home country in the form of dividends to investors. Government revenues from taxation on profits also increase.

26 Aid can be supplied through three main systems:

- **bilaterally**, with aid given from one government to another
- **multilaterally**, when money is given by governments to international organisations to assist programmes in poorer nations (World Bank, UNESCO)
- **NGOs**, many of which are charities (e.g. Oxfam, Merlin and Comic Relief), distribute aid in a variety of ways

27 Aid can be distributed in various forms such as food, goods, technical assistance and construction. It can be distributed through:

- **short-term aid** — countries and organisations respond to a disaster, such as the earthquake in Haiti, 2010
- **long-term development projects** such as agriculture, irrigation, power supply, education and medical facilities
- **'top-down' aid**, in which the responsible body directs operations from above, such as when building irrigation schemes through dams or barrages
- **'bottom-up schemes'** in which organisations work with the people in receipt of the aid, using local knowledge to bring about change

28 **Trade** promotes economic growth which is essential to economic development. More wealth is generated allowing living standards to rise. Against this, critics have pointed out that:

- LDCs cannot be competitive in global markets because they cannot invest in industrial and technological development as do richer countries
- many poorer countries depend upon the export of agricultural goods the price of which fluctuates; richer countries may protect their farmers through subsidies
- wealth generated by trade does not always 'trickle down' to the majority of the population
- the debts of LDCs are too great to be overcome easily

Aid helps people and can be directed towards economic, humanitarian, social and environmental development. Critics have observed that:

- aid does not always reach those people who need it most
- countries lacking basic infrastructure find it difficult to use aid effectively
- aid dependency can be created — it becomes a substantial part of national income
- aid often comes with strings attached — the recipient may have to accept conditions laid down by the donor

29 **Economic sustainability** is the ability of economies to sustain themselves when resources decline (or become too expensive to exploit) and when the population dependent upon those resources is increasing.

Environmental sustainability seeks to maintain ecological processes and life-support systems, preserve genetic diversity and ensure the utilisation of species and ecosystems without destroying them.

30 Sustainable tourism is tourism that does not set out to destroy what it sets out to explore. When tourist flow increases, tourism can cause major environmental problems. This means that, unless successful management strategies are evolved, the cost of tourism can soon outweigh the benefits.

Sustainable tourism is an industry committed to making a low impact on the natural environment and local culture, while helping to generate income and employment for local people. Ecotourism is a form of sustainable tourism, as it seeks to conserve the environment for future generations. Within this, environmental and sociological interests have to be balanced against purely economic aims. Ecotourism has been developed largely by small, independent tour companies, and today constitutes less than 5% of the tourism market.

Contemporary conflicts and challenges

1 A conflict resulting from nationalism is the product of extreme loyalty and devotion to a sovereign country. Examples include Scottish and Welsh nationalism, or at the more violent extreme, that concerning Serbia after the break-up of the former Yugoslavia. Regionalism refers to consciousness of a homogeneous area within one or more countries. Examples of regionalism include the Basques of Spain and France, and the Kurds of Turkey, Iraq, Iran and Syria.

2 **Ethnicity** refers to the grouping of people according to their ethnic origins or characteristics. An example of conflict based on this is the civil war in Rwanda where the Hutu and Tutsi tribes fought. **Territory** refers to a geographic area belonging to, or under the jurisdiction of, a governmental authority. The conflict in Western Sahara illustrates this, where both Morocco and Mauritania claim the territory. **Ideology** is a systematic body of concepts regarding human life or culture. The conflict in Afghanistan between the Taliban and the US, UK and Pakistan forces is an example of this type of conflict.

3 There are four main scales of conflict in the world:
- international — conflict involves the participation of more than one country

- national — conflict takes place within a country
- regional — conflict takes place within an area of one country, or across the borders of one or more countries
- local — conflict is restricted to a small part of one region of a country

4 **Terrorism** refers to the systematic use of terror as a means of coercion to a political, or more frequently an ideological, end. **Insurrection** is an act or instance of revolt against either a civil authority or an established government and usually involves rebellion against the rules of that government.

5 **Invasion** is the hostile encroachment on to the land of another sovereign country. The occupation of Kuwait in August 1990 by Iraqi troops is an example. **Ethnic cleansing** was the term given to the enforced movement of non-Serbian people from their land and houses in Bosnia Herzegovina and Croatia by the Serbs after the collapse of the former Yugoslavia. Some 40 000 Bosnian Muslims in Srebrenica were then targeted for extinction. They were killed deliberately and methodically solely on the basis of their identity.

6 The eventual persuasion of UK governments to grant devolved power to the Welsh and Scottish parliaments is a good example.

7 Within the UK, most conflicts over the use of land at a local level are resolved by reference to planning authorities. An application is made initially to the local authority planning officer who then decides whether to award planning permission. If permission is refused then the applicant can appeal to the local planning committee and, if unsuccessful there, to DEFRA. A developer could be asked to make modifications to the original proposal or to provide additional facilities to make the proposal more acceptable to the public and/or council.

8 The United Nations (UN) was founded to prevent and resolve international conflicts and to help build a culture of peace in the world. These intentions are transferred into action by the different agencies, departments and programmes within the umbrella of the UN. Under its supervision, specialised programmes and agencies such as the UN Development Programme (UNDP), the UN Educational, Scientific and Cultural Organization (UNESCO), the UN Environment Programme (UNEP), the UN High Commissioner for Human

Rights (UNHCHR), the UN Institute for Disarmament Research (UNIDIR), are trying to prevent deadly conflicts from proliferating by attacking the roots of the conflicts, and not only the acts of violence that are the symptoms. Blue-helmeted UN forces, made up of soldiers from contributing nations, are involved in policing activities in conflict zones around the world.

9 Any question based on this area of the specification is likely to follow this logical pattern: why has the conflict arisen; what do various people think about it; how can it be resolved? The key aspect is that you ground your response with a clear sense of place. The more local information you can give the better. You should give the precise reasons for the conflict having developed, i.e. what caused some people to want the proposal to go ahead, and why some people objected to it. You should refer to groups and/ or individuals who have views on the conflict by name and make it clear why they hold their particular views. It is often the case that groups who are united in either being in favour of, or against, a proposal have different reasons for their stance. Make sure that you make these variations clear as this will enable a higher mark to be awarded. You should also be aware of the precise possible (or actual) outcomes of the conflict and be able to assess the degree to which the participants will benefit, or lose, once the outcomes are in place.

10 The key word in this question is 'environmental'. You must endeavour to keep your answer focused on this element of the conflict. An example could be in Darfur:

> Darfur is a semi-arid province in the west of Sudan. Arab Janjaweed have been accused of riding into the villages of the black African people, attacking them and setting fire to the villages. As a result, the women and their children have left the villages and their land in order to go to somewhere that is safe. They have settled near the main towns of the area, where food, water and medical help are being provided by charities. The environmental costs are many. The former villages now stand idle, many in burnt ruins. The plots of land around them are untended and are reverting back to some form of natural vegetation. The area is on the edge of the Sahara desert and drought-resistant plants are being re-established. Many of these plants have long roots and once established they are

difficult to remove. The former farmland is also going to ruin. Around the refugee camps the people continue to try and find fuelwood for cooking and heating. Areas of woodland are disappearing fast.

11 The key words in this question are 'standard of living'. You must endeavour to keep your answer focused on this element of the conflict. An example could be in Afghanistan:

> In Afghanistan, the standard of living of the inhabitants is very low. The political systems that operate in the country are responsible for holding it back both socially and economically. When the Taliban took over in 1996, educational and career opportunities for girls and women ended. In 2000, 89% of the female population aged over 14 had no schooling at all, 6% had attended primary school and 4%, secondary school. Only 1.3% had been to university. Few opportunities meant girls stayed at home and could not work outside the home as adults. Under the Taliban, a woman's place was in the home, girls' schools were closed and professional women (teachers, lecturers, doctors etc.) were no longer allowed to work. Women had no access to medical attention, as male doctors were not allowed to treat them. In the twenty-first century, conditions are slowly improving, especially in the large cities. There is better healthcare, and education is improving under the new regime, which is supported by aid from the West and guaranteed by western troops. Progress, however, is slow.

12 The key word in this question is the word 'economy'. You must endeavour to keep your answer focused on this element of the conflict. An example could be in the Gaza Strip:

> The Gaza Strip is one of the occupied territories to the southwest of Israel. The economic impacts of the conflict are as follows:
> - The area's chief economic problem is the extreme poverty of the large number of Palestinian Arab refugees living there.
> - It is one of the most crowded areas of the world. Unemployment is high, people are poor and the economy is crippled by an international boycott and by Israel withholding desperately needed Palestinian tax revenues.

- Foreign powers, Israel and Egypt, control Gaza's borders, opening and closing them at will.
- Despite frequently announced cease-fires between differing factions, street battles in Gaza are common place, preventing people going about their lives and crippling investment in the area.
- In December 2008 and January 2009 the area was bombarded by the Israeli army. Economic life came to a standstill as homes and businesses were destroyed. Outside investment in the area ceased and Gaza is now totally dependent on aid from overseas.

13 A **multicultural society** is a social grouping that contains members from a wide variety of national, linguistic, religious and/or cultural backgrounds. It is often an emotive issue, especially when 'cultural' differences are interpreted as racial differences. Although skin colour remains as a visible distinguishing feature, people differ from one another in terms of ethnicity, language, religion and culture. Multicultural societies are the result of migration, both forced and voluntary. They may also generate movement as persecuted minorities seek to escape oppression.

14 Multicultural societies are largely formed by migration. There have been a number of significant migrations into the UK over the last 200 years. The descendants of these immigrants, and the inter-marriage that has taken place subsequently, have created the multicultural society that now exists. The main migrations that have taken place into the UK are:

- nineteenth century: Jewish arrivals from Russia and Poland, and Irish from rural Ireland
- 1930s and Second World War: further movements of Jews and Poles
- 1948–1960s: black Caribbean workers and Asians from India, Pakistan and Bangladesh, working mainly in public services and textile industries
- 1970s: East African Asians (from Uganda) and Vietnamese
- 1980–90s: Eastern European refugees from political unrest in Romania and the former Yugoslavia
- 2000s: economic migration from eastern European countries such as Poland

There has been considerable inter-mixing of these communities in the last 30 years, especially in cities such as Leicester, Birmingham, the towns and cities of Yorkshire and Lancashire, and the London area.

15 The Asian population is concentrated in the central parts of the city with marked reductions in density to the south and east. However, to the north and west of the city there are significant numbers as far as the ring road. The only areas of concentration beyond the ring road are to the north of the city.

16 The geographical distribution of black Caribbean people has changed over time. In the 1960s, when many such people came to the UK, they were concentrated in inner-city areas such as Chapeltown in Leeds where the available housing was cheap. In addition, they tended to congregate together because prejudice by landlords was prevalent at that time. As attitudes changed (partly due to legislation) and incomes increased, black Caribbean people and their descendants have moved into more suburban and affluent areas. Such movements have been largely due to income changes and aspirational factors. However, some parts of the UK still have concentrations of black Caribbean people, for example Moss Side in Manchester, and Lambeth and Southwark in London.

17 It is important that not only are you specific in the nature of the issues identified but that you relate them to an area(s) affected. One issue is the variation in educational attainment among ethnic groups. There is some evidence to suggest that children from black Caribbean backgrounds (as in south London) are underachieving compared not only with the white population but also with other ethnic groups. Conversely, the performance of children from Indian, Pakistani (as in West Yorkshire) and Chinese backgrounds appears, on average, to be better than that of white children. Ofsted has stated that the white 'working-class' male is currently the lowest achiever in schools.

Religious tension is an extreme issue. In 2001, Bradford was the centre of a race riot carried out by the Indian and Pakistani community over the activities of the BNP in the area. Religious intolerance has become prominent in the years since 2001 due to the activities of Muslim terrorists, which has led to an escalation of suspicion and hatred of the Muslim faith. This has been found in areas such as Finsbury Park in London.

18 One significant benefit that can be attributed to the multicultural society in the UK is the wide range of food types and outlets in the country. Most high streets now have Italian, Chinese and Indian restaurants, added to more recently by Mexican, Thai and even Polish. This is typified by the rise of the popularity of the dish chicken tikka masala. Its invention has been attributed to a chef in Glasgow and attempts have been made to have the EU grant the dish Protected Designation of Origin status as a Glaswegian dish. Surveys have found chicken tikka masala to be the most popular meal in British restaurants and it has been called 'Britain's true national dish'.

19 **Separatism** refers to the attempts by regional groups to gain more political control from central government over the area in which they live. For some groups, the ideal would be total independence. **Autonomy** is the right of self-government.

20 Three areas where separatist pressures exist are:
- northern Spain/southwest France — the Basque area
- southern Russia — the area known as Chechnya
- southeast Turkey/northern Iran and Iraq — the Kurdish area

21 Reasons for separatist pressure in a region include:
- an area that is economically depressed compared with a wealthier core
- a minority language or culture or religious grouping with a different history
- the perception that exploitation of local resources by national government results in little economic gain for the region
- peripheral location to the economic/political core
- collapse of the state, weakening the political power that held the regions together (e.g. the former USSR and Yugoslavia)
- the strengthening of supranational bodies such as the EU, which has led many nationalist groups to think that they have a better chance of developing economically if they are independent

22 In Spain, a Basque nationalist organisation, ETA (Euskadi ta Askatasuna), was formed, which declared war on the Spanish state in the 1960s. ETA has operated a violent campaign, targeting police, security forces, and legal and government figures and buildings. The ETA campaign of bombing has continued sporadically since 2002 with attacks along the Costa del Sol and Majorca, targeting the Spanish tourist trade.

In Scotland, the Scottish National Party (SNP) has independence as its central tenet and it has campaigned politically for this. This drive was partly satisfied by the establishment in 1999 of a devolved parliament with limited tax-raising powers. In 2007, the SNP became the largest party in the Scottish Parliament, and is now demanding a referendum on the issue.

23 Poverty can be measured by the international poverty line. This is based on a level of consumption representative of the poverty lines found in low-income countries. In 2008, the international poverty line was set at $1.25 a day, measured in terms of 1993 purchasing power parity (PPP). Poverty can also be measured by the human development index (HDI) which combines the variables of life expectancy, educational attainment and real GDP per capita.

24 The figure illustrates well the divide between developed and developing countries. There is high internet usage in western Europe, North America and Australia. Usage is rare in most of Africa and in southwestern and southeastern Asia. However, there are interesting anomalies — high usage in China and Brazil and lower usage in parts of eastern Europe. The relationship is complex.

25 The causes of poverty are complex and interrelated. It is caused by a low income, which contributes to poor nutrition and health. Education levels, including literacy, are key indicators of poverty; areas with low school enrolment tend to be poor. Such areas also have little economic diversification — they are dependent on the export of commodities that are subject to price variations. As well as economic vulnerability, many poor areas are subject to natural hazards. LDCs are very much dependent on external finance and are subject to high levels of international debt.

26 In most areas shown the proportion of people living in poverty has fallen, and collectively in the developing world it has almost halved. However, the MDG target has not been reached collectively. The reduction has been most rapid in eastern Asia where the fall has taken the proportion involved well below the MDG target — the only area to achieve this level of reduction. However, the proportion in poverty in western Asia has increased, which may reflect the problems in Iraq and Afghanistan. The area that has

seen the least fall is sub-Saharan Africa — the area with the worst problem. This area is still a long way from the MDG target.

27 The G8 countries are the richest countries in the world: Japan, USA, Germany, France, Canada, UK, Italy and Russia. At the Gleneagles summit in 2005, and at the UN World Summit later that year, G8 donors committed to increasing their aid to developing countries to 0.7% of gross national income. However, with most Western economies in recession, even fulfilment of those commitments implies a diminished amount of aid. For many developing countries, less aid would not only impede further progress, it could reverse some of the gains already made.

28 The four countries shown are at different levels of development. Economic prosperity and the wealth to invest in making progress will be a big factor, as for example in Brazil.

However, despite being a poor country, Bangladesh has made some progress. Small-scale development projects, such as tube wells and microcredit, seem to have had a considerable impact. The scale of the problems, particularly the huge population, could be a reason why the wealth generated by economic growth in India is not trickling down through its society. Political will could be seen as crucial to pushing through the improvements needed. Help in the form of aid, or hindrance in the form of debt, might be important in allowing some countries to be more successful than others. Some specific measures, such as gender equality, might be held back by

cultural values (as in Egypt) and taboos about diseases such as HIV/AIDS. A focus on some areas might lead to losing track of others, such as the lack of health progress in Bangladesh. Frequent hazards might create a one-step forward, two-steps back situation.

29 The key aspect of this question is to provide information that is clearly applicable to the area chosen. An example could be Afghanistan. On an almost daily basis news comes from Afghanistan of suicide bombings in the cities, such as Kabul, and roadside bombs in the countryside, killing soldiers and civilians alike. The country has tried to hold free elections, but with great difficulty due to the lack of security. Development of industry, improvements to homes and transport systems, and the provision of basic facilities such as clean water and sewerage, education and health is being held back by the insecurity of the situation. Where possible, you should give examples of actual events and consequences.

30 The key aspect of this question is to provide information that is clearly applicable to the area chosen. An example could be Croatia. One way to reduce the threat of further civil strife in this country has been for the Croatian government to encourage economic development of the west of the country. An example is the provision of a new motorway stretching from Zagreb to Dubrovnik, thereby encouraging greater investment in the coastal area. In addition, funds from the EU, Turkey and Russia are being sought to improve the number and quality of hotels in the area, so as to attract more tourists.

A

ablation 7, 9
abrasion 2, 7, 11, 17
accumulation 7, 9
acid rain 31
adaptations by vegetation and animals to
    climate 53, 56
age, and health 37, 41
age structure 25, 26, 36
agribusinesses 27, 30
agricultural production 27, 28
aid 63, 64, 67
air masses, British Isles 46, 47, 50
air quality, urban areas 47
alluvial fans 16
alpine environments 6
Antarctica 6, 10
anticyclones 46, 47, 50, 51
appropriate technology 29, 31
arches 11
Arctic ice, melting of 49
arêtes 6
aridisols 16, 18
aridity 17, 18
Asian Tiger economies 63, 65
asthenosphere 42, 44
atmosphere 46, 48
atmospheric heat budget 46
autonomy (national) 71

B

badlands 16, 19
bahada 19
Bangalore, India 60
barchans 16–17, 19
barrages 12
bars (coastal) 11
base flow 3
bays 11, 15
beaches 11, 14
beach nourishment 12, 15
berms 11
biodiversity 53–4, 56
biomass 31, 34
birth rate 20, 22, 23
blow holes 11
buffer zones 29
buttes 16

C

capacity, river 1, 4
capital flows 63
carbon dioxide emissions 30
carbon footprint 52
channel characteristics 1, 5
charitable organisations 40
chemical weathering 17, 18
China 63, 64, 65
cholera 38
cliffs 11, 15
climate 46–52
climatic change 47, 48, 52

climatic climax 53, 55
climatic controls 47
coal 34
coastal deposition 11
coastal environments 11–15
coastal erosion 11, 12, 14
coastal flooding 14
coastal landforms 11, 13–15
coastal management 15
coastal protection 12, 14
cold environments 6–10
colonisation of wasteland 54, 56
command words vi–vii
Common Agricultural Policy (CAP) 29
competence, river 1, 4
composite volcanoes 42, 45
conflict resolution 68, 70
conflicts 67–73
conservative margins 42, 45
constructive margins 42
constructive waves 11, 13
consumption, patterns of 63
contemporary conflicts 67–73
continental drift 44
continental plates 42, 44, 45
convergent margins 44–5
cool temperate western maritime (CTWM)
    46, 50, 51
corries 6, 7, 9
counterurbanisation 57, 58, 59, 60, 61
Cuba, health 39
cultural groupings, UK 68, 71
culture 67
cusps 11
cyclones 47, 51

D

death rate 20, 23
debate, political 68, 70
decentralisation of retailing 58, 62
deflation hollows 16
deforestation 1
deltas 1, 5
demand for food 27
demographic transition model (DTM) 20,
    21, 23
dependency ratios 24
depressions 46, 47, 50, 51
desert climate 16
desertification 16, 18, 19–20
destructive margins 42, 45
destructive waves 11, 13
developing countries and energy 35
development 62–7, 72
development continuum 63, 65
development gap 65
development issues, biome 53
disease and death rate 23
diseases of affluence 37, 38, 39
diurnal range of temperature 16, 18
divergent margins see constructive margins
drainage basin hydrological cycle 1, 3
drumlins 6, 10

Dubai 64
dumping, food trade 28
dune regeneration 12
dunes see sand dunes

E

Earth, structure of 42
earthquakes 42, 43, 44, 45, 46
ecological conservation 54, 56
ecological responses to climate 53
economic and environmental sustainability
    63, 64, 67
economic development 16, 23, 57–8, 59,
    64
ecosystems 52–7
ecotourism 63
education 23, 36
electricity, UK 34
emergent coastlines 11, 14
employment 25, 26
energy conservation 31, 35
energy consumption, world 32, 33
energy flows 52
energy issues 31–6
energy management 36
energy production 31, 32, 35
energy use, and environment 35
englacial transport 6
environmental stewardship 29
environment and conflict 70
environment and health 36
ephemerals 16, 18
eskers 6
ethnic cleansing 70
ethnicity and conflict 67, 69
ethnic population distribution 25–6
EU
    food 27, 29
    growth of 63, 65, 66
eustatic sea-level change 12, 14
evapotranspiration 1, 3, 18
exam skills jigsaw vi
exam technique v–vi
exogenous rivers 16, 19
extrusive volcanic landforms 42

F

fair trade 28
famine, periodic 36, 37, 39
fertility rate 20, 22
flash flooding 17, 19
flooding, in desert regions 16
flood management strategies 3
floodplains 1, 5
flood prediction 3, 5
floods 1–5
flow resources 31, 32
fluvial deposition 1, 4
fluvial erosion 1, 2, 4
fluvioglacial processes 6, 8, 10
fog 46, 47
food chains 52
food consumption 27

food production 27
food supply 27
food trade 27
food transport 30
food webs 52, 55
foreign direct investment (FDI) 65, 67
fossil fuels 31, 33
fragile environments 6, 10, 53, 54, 56, 57
fronts (weather) 46, 47, 50
frost shattering 7, 10
fuelwood 18, 31, 34

G

G8 68, 72
gabions 12
gas-fired power stations 34
GDP 62, 65
gender, and health care 37, 41
general atmospheric circulation 46
genetic modification (GM) of crops 29
gentrification 57, 61
geopolitics
  of energy 31
  of food 27
Gersmehl diagram 52, 56
glacial budget 6, 7
glacial deposition 6, 7, 10
glacial environments 6
glacial erosion 6, 7, 9
glacial meltwater 8
glacial transportation 6, 7, 10
glacial troughs 6, 10
glaciers 6, 9
global agricultural production 28
global atmospheric system 18
globalisation 62–7
global marketing 63, 65
global patterns of energy 31, 33
global trade and environment 27
global warming 5, 47, 48, 52
GNP 62
gorges 1
graded profiles 1
Green Revolution 27, 28, 29
groupings of nations 63, 64, 66
growth hormones 29
groynes 12

H

Hadley cells 46, 48
halosere 53
hanging valleys 6
hard engineering 3, 5, 12, 14
headlands 11, 13, 15
health, regional variations in UK 36
health care approaches 36, 37, 40
health issues 36–41
Health Profiles, PCT 40–1
heather moorland 53, 54
high-yielding varieties (HYV) 29
HIV/AIDS 38
Hjulström curve 2
hot desert environments 16–20

hot spots 42, 45
housing provision 25
Hull, floods 5
human activity
  and deserts 16, 20
  and ecosystems 53, 54, 55, 56
  and tundra 6, 8, 10
human development index (HDI) 62
hunger 24
hurricanes 47, 51
hydraulic radius 5
hydrograph 1, 4
hydrological cycle 1
hydrosere 53

I

ice flows 6, 7, 8
ice movement 8
ice sheets 8
ice wedges 6
identity and conflict 67
ideology and conflict 67, 69
incised meanders 1, 5
income 36
India 63, 65, 66, 67
infant mortality 22
infectious diseases 37, 38
inselbergs 16
insurrection 68, 69
integrated pest management 29
interception 3
international agencies 68
international conflict 69, 70
internet users 71
inter-tropical convergence zone (ITCZ) 46, 47, 51
intrusive volcanic landforms 42
invasion and conflict 70
isostatic sea-level change 12, 14

K

kames 6
kettle holes 6
key geographical terms x
key words vii–ix
kinetic energy 1
knickpoints 1
Komodo National Park, Indonesia 56–7

L

labour flows 63
lahars 42, 45
land colonisation 29
land reform 29
land use management 12
latitude and climate 47, 48, 49
least developed countries (LDCs) 62, 64, 66
levées 1
lithosere 53
lithosphere 42, 44
local conflict 67, 68, 70
localism 67

local produce 30
locational knowledge ix–x
long profiles 1, 5
longshore drift 11, 14
lowland glaciation 10

M

malnutrition 36, 37, 39
manufacturing, global distribution 65, 66
marsh creation 12
mass movement (coastal) 12
maternal mortality 37
Matterhorn 9
meanders 1
mechanical weathering 17, 18
mega cities 57, 59
meltwater channels 6
mesas 16
migration 20, 21, 24, 25
Millennium Development Goals (MDGs) 68, 72
millionaire cities 57, 59
moraines 6, 10
morbidity 36, 37, 40
mortality 36, 37
multicultural societies 68, 70–1

N

national conflict 67
National Health Service 39
nationalism 67, 69
natural gas 33, 34
neve 8
newly industrialised countries (NICs) 63, 65
NGOs 68
Nissan 66
nivation 10
nivation hollows 6
non-communicable diseases 37, 38, 39
non-renewable resources 31
non-violent conflict 68
North–South divide 63, 64
nuclear power 31, 34, 35
nutrient cycling 52, 56

O

obesity 36, 37, 39
occupation type 36
oceanic circulation 46, 49
oceanic plates 42, 44
oil 33, 34, 35
OPEC 33
organic farming 30
out-of-town retailing areas 62
outwash plains 6, 10
overpopulation 24
overproduction 29
oxbow lakes 1

P

palaeomagnetism 43, 44
particulate pollution 47, 52

partnership schemes 57, 61
patterned ground 6
pediments 16
periglacial environments 6, 8
periglaciation 6, 8
periodic famine 36, 37, 39
permafrost 6, 10
petroleum TNCs 35
pharmaceutical TNCs 36, 40
photochemical smog 47, 52
pingos 6
plagioclimax 53, 54, 55, 56
planning and urbanisation 58
plate tectonics 42
plucking 7
Poland 23
polar environments 6
political activity 68
pollution 36, 47, 48
pollution reduction policies 47, 48, 52
population and resources 20, 21, 24
population change 20–6
population control 25
population decline 25
population density 23
population growth 23, 25, 28
population indicators 20
population pyramids 23
population structures 21, 23
potential energy 1
potholes 1, 2
poverty 66, 68, 71–2
Primary Care Trusts (PCTs) 40
primary energy mix 31, 32
product flows 63
production and distribution, globalisation
    of 36, 63
pro-glacial lakes 6
property-led regeneration 57, 61
psammosere 53
pyramidal peaks 6

Q
quotas 29

R
radiation fog 46, 47
rainforest 56
rapids 1
recycling 62
redevelopment schemes 58, 61
reg 19
regeneration of urban areas 57, 58, 61
regional conflict 67, 69
regionalism 67, 69
rejuvenation, river 1, 2, 5
renewable resources 31
resources, used in exams x
resources and conflict 67, 68, 70
retailing 58, 62
re-urbanisation 57, 58, 59, 61
revetments 12, 15
revision strategies xi–xii

ribbon lakes 6
Richter scale 46
rift valley 42, 44
rip-rap 12, 15
river discharge 2, 4
river flooding 5
river load 2
river rejuvenation 1, 2, 5
rivers 1–5
river terraces 1
river transport 1, 4
roches moutonnées 6, 10
rock pedestals 16, 19
routeway ecologies 54, 56
runnels 11
runoff 1, 12, 19
rural areas 21, 25, 52
rural–urban fringe 54, 56

S
Sahel 20
salt lakes 16
salt marshes 11, 15
sand dunes
    coastal 11, 15
    desert 16–17, 19
sea-floor spreading 43, 44
sea-level change 12, 14
sea walls 12
secondary energy 31, 32
security 69, 72
sediment cells 11, 13
sediment roundness 4
sediment sources 11
seismic events 43
seismic waves 46
separatism 68, 69, 71
service flows 63
service sector 63, 64, 67
set aside 29
shield volcanoes 42, 45
snow line 8
social welfare 26
soft engineering 3, 5, 12, 14, 15
soil liquefaction 42, 46
soil moisture budget 53, 56
solar power 31, 33
solifluction 10
solifluction lobes 6
spits 11, 14
stacks 11
stock resources 31, 32
storm events, British Isles 46, 47, 51
storm hydrograph 1, 4
stratopause 46
stratosphere 46
sub-aerial weathering 12, 14
subduction 43, 44, 45
subglacial transport 6
submergent coastlines 11, 14
subsidies 29
subsistence agriculture 28
suburbanisation 57, 58, 59, 60, 61

succession 53, 55, 56
supraglacial transport 6
sustainability
    biome 53–4, 56
    economic and environmental 63, 64, 67
    transport 35
    urban areas 58
sustainable development 6, 31
sustainable energy supplies 31
sustainable food supplies 27, 30
sustainable tourism 64, 67
synoptic charts 51

T
temperate deciduous woodland biome 53,
    55
territory and conflict 67, 69
terrorism 68, 69
Thailand 23
third world 62, 65
tidal energy 31, 34
tides 11, 15
timing in exams x–xi
TNCs
    agriculture 27
    and development 63, 64, 66, 67
    energy 32
    petroleum 34, 35
    pharmaceutical 36, 40
    tobacco 36, 40
tourism 10, 20, 64, 67
trade 63, 64, 67
tradition, and birth rate 23
transform faults 44
transnational corporations *see* TNCs
transport 58, 62
transport and sustainability 35
trophic levels 52, 55
tropical biomes 53, 56
tropical climates 47
tropical revolving storms 47, 48, 51
tropopause 46
troposphere 46
tsunamis 42, 43, 45, 46
tundra 6, 8, 10
typhoons 47, 51

U
UK food transport 30
undernourishment 24–5, 39
underpopulation 24
United Nations 68
upper atmospheric circulation 46
urban areas 21, 52
urban climate 47, 48
urban decline 57, 58, 61
urban heat island effect 47, 51–2
urbanisation 1, 54, 57–8, 59, 60
urban niche 56
urban regeneration 57, 58, 61
urban winds 47, 52
USA, health 39

V

valley cross profiles   1
vegetation, desert   16, 18
ventifacts   16
volcanic activity   42–6
vulcanicity   42–6

W

wadis   16, 19
war   68
waste management   58, 62
water balance   1, 2, 3
water budget graph   3
water deposition, desert   16, 17
water erosion, desert   16, 17
waterfalls   1
wave-cut platforms   11, 15
wave energy   31, 34
wave erosion   14
wealth   25, 26, 37, 41, 46
weather   46–52
Wegener, Alfred   44
wilderness areas   6
wind deposition   17
wind energy   31, 33
wind erosion   16, 17, 19
wind farms   34
wind transportation, desert   17, 19
world cities   57–62
World Food Summit (WFS)   24

X

xerophytes   16, 18

Y

yardangs   16
youthful populations   24

Z

zeugen   16